TOWARD A POSITIVE PSYCHOLOGY OF RELIGION

This is a brilliant work. The ideas in this book are revolutionary. Robert Rocco Cottone has produced a work that is destined to be a classic. He has merged ideas from the Positive Psychology movement, ethics, postmodern philosophy, and religion into a vision of religion for the future. He skillfully guides readers through complex ideas – infusing humor, personal stories, and student-teacher dialogues to make the ideas lively and accessible. Each chapter builds and extends the reader's understanding. Then, at the end, he makes the case for a new religious order. Science and religion are reconciled. A truth is defined. And the reader is left filled with hope along with a new, postmodern under-standing of religion.

Dr. Mark Pope, Past President and Fellow of the American Counseling Association. Fellow of the American Psychological Association

This book is provocative, enlightening, and affirming of our deepest social need to connect spiritually with others. Robert Rocco Cottone critiques the ancient religions and atheism in a way that will likely arouse believers of these traditions. Rather than being unsettling, his analysis is eye-opening and inviting. He adds to his critique an alter-native, unique, and positive way of understanding religion and belief. The blending of Positive Psychology and postmodern philosophy is refreshing and groundbreaking. This book represents a call for a new ethical movement in religion — toward a positive psychology of religion. You will never view religion the same again.

Vilia Tarvydas, Ph.D., Professor of Counseling, Rehabilitation and Student Development at the University of Iowa and the Director of the Institute on Rehabilitation and Disability Ethics.

It is difficult for thinking people to embrace a spiritual life when the history of religion from Biblical to modern times shows so many power grabs, parochial interests, wars and excommunications. How can everyone be right, when each claims to be? And why do we witness such strife and hard-headed control from faith leaders? Professor Robert Rocco Cottone, in his new book, Toward a Positive Psychology of Religion: Belief Science in the Postmodern Era, asks us not to throw the baby out with the bath water, because he believes that a healthy contemporary spirituality is emerging. He introduces the reader to postmodern religion, which is a spirituality based on the inherent meaning that we all intuit in human relationships. Cottone tells us how he found his way from a Roman Catholic upbringing to find a liberating sense of meaning in an adult sense of Godliness. He guides us with the vigor of a man who loves his faith and wants others to at least understand it. Academics will find this book satisfying because Professor Cottone covers his bases brilliantly, from the Bible to Maturana to Kuhn. For the lay public, he offers a way out of a constricted sense of religion, with a postmodern ethic and commitment to love. This book is the postmodern credo from theory to practice; it is a great accomplishment.

Mark R. Banschick, M.D., Child and Adolescent Psychiatrist
Adjunct Professor – Hebrew Union College

In a time when post-modern discourse could make even an academician's head spin, Dr. Cottone applies this discipline to a study of religion in a down-to-earth, easy-to-read style that even philosophically weak-kneed people will enjoy. He explores a wide gamut of important and fascinating issues in religion, with conclusions that extend beyond the intellectual realm and into the practical dilemmas of everyday living. This is a must-read for anyone interested in the philosophy and psychology of religious studies.

John Suler, Ph.D., Professor of Psychology, Rider University

Toward a Positive Psychology of Religion: Belief Science in the Postmodern Era

Toward a Positive Psychology of Religion: Belief Science in the Postmodern Era

Robert Rocco Cottone

BOOKS

Winchester, UK
Washington, USA

First published by O-Books, 2011
O-Books is an imprint of John Hunt Publishing Ltd., Laurel House, Station Approach,
Alresford, Hants, SO24 9JH, UK
office1@o-books.net
www.o-books.com

For distributor details and how to order please visit the 'Ordering' section on our website.

Text copyright Robert Rocco Cottone 2010

ISBN: 978 1 84694 429 1

A CIP catalogue record for this book is available from the British Library.

Design: Stuart Davies

Printed and bound by CPI Group (UK) Ltd, Croydon, CR0 4YY

We operate a distinctive and ethical publishing philosophy in all
areas of our business, from our global network of authors to
production and worldwide distribution.

CONTENTS

This book is dedicated to my best friends, who have stood by me with love and understanding even as I have challenged their fundamental beliefs. I hold their friendships precious.

Preface

This book has been a labor of love. I have never written a book for the popular press, and I have found the experience personally rewarding. This work, in many ways, is a culmination of a life of study of psychology, counseling, religion, and ethics. The journey started early in childhood as I experienced strong religious feelings and a close connection to my religious community. A turning point came near the end of my college days when I began to question my religion and to consider alternative views. In 1974 I naively felt I had it "all figured out" as a graduate student in counseling. I had much to learn. I now believe I have a better understanding of one of many religious viewpoints. For whatever reason, I feel compelled to share that viewpoint with you.

I claim no ownership of these ideas. These ideas have come from others – through my relationships as a man, a son, a husband, a father, a student, a teacher, and a friend. I owe many people for what is contained in these pages. Most importantly, readers will recognize the ideas of Gregory Bateson, Humberto Maturana, Kenneth Gergen, and other social, systemic, and postmodern theorists. The works of Maturana (1978, 1980) and Gergen (1985, 2001) are highlighted in this book. Gergen published a seminal work on application of postmodern philosophy to psychology (Gergen, 1985), and since this book is more a personal exposition than a scholarly thesis, I have relied only on a few referenced works. Readers are referred to the publications of Gergen, who provides a thorough historical review, in order to connect his work to the postmodern intellectual movement in general. Those ideas pass through his works and through the arguments made in this book. This book, therefore, is really a reflection of the work of postmodern theorists, and I give them full credit. I also credit ethicists in adding to this book's theme—the works of Beauchamp and Childress, Kitchener, Tarvydas, and others live through the ideas in this work. My good friend Vilia Tarvydas has taught me much on issues of ethics and decision making, and her contribution is significant in that regard. And, of course, the work of Seligman and Csikszentmihalyi (2000) in establishing the "positive psychology" movement, and the movement itself, have had a major influence on the ideas in this book. My contribution to the ideas in this book is really about synthesis—I hold no patent to these ideas, but I am proud to be able to organize them in the form of a religious philosophy. I hope you find the ideas compelling.

In this book I will address the most practiced religions. It is estimated that there are thousands of religions, but the majority of people on earth practice just a few religions: Christianity, Islam, Hinduism, Buddhism, Judaism, and atheism/agnosticism. I offer my apologies to the other religions. And I offer apologies to the religions that I do address, as my assessments of them are at times quite critical and non-complimentary. They are ancient traditions, and this book addresses religion from the perspective of the postmodern era, a period of time and a philosophy that challenges the ideals of ancient times and of modernism. As a former practicing Roman Catholic, I am a bit more critical, and at times more complimentary, of Roman Catholicism than any other religion or religious denomination, primarily because I have greater acquaintance with Roman Catholic doctrine. However, as readers will come to understand by the end of this book, I respect all religious traditions, even when I have serious doctrinal disagreements with them. I certainly value the powerful and healthy relationships I experienced through the Roman Catholic Church, as my experience with practicing Catholics has shown me that they are part of a very loving, giving, and profoundly religious community—the type of community that all religions should aspire to create.

I owe a special thanks to my two oldest children, Christopher and Kristina Cottone, for being patient with me and for valuing my effort to put forth these ideas. In a sense, I did this for them and for their younger siblings, who someday may come to understand the ideas presented here. I owe much to my very devoutly Roman Catholic wife, Molly, who has been patient with me through my religious reawakening and tolerant of views that sometimes challenge her most fundamental beliefs. I also owe a special thanks to Dr. Jim Lane, who was the first to officially join me in holding faith in the set of principles put forth in this text. His support has been affirming. He is an incredible friend. My special friend and colleague Matthew Lemberger has been encouraging and especially helpful bringing me to understand the Hindu faith and Hindu tradition. Mark Pope, Donna McCall, Brian Hutchison, and Carl Bassi have offered counsel, constructive criticism, and education on matters of religious doctrine and tradition, and I sincerely appreciate their help. My sister Debra and my cousins James and Marie Donato have also supported me, and their encouragement is very special and valuable to me. I could not have done this without the help of these tolerant and understanding people. They are my little circle of support as I have explored the nature of religious belief and the process of believing. I hope to expand that circle of support by sharing with you my most profound understanding of my experiences from a postmodern religious perspective.

I wish you well on your journey.

ɡ৯৯

Part I:

Postmodern Religion, Relationships,
and Ethics

ɡ৯৯

Chapter One

Introduction: Understanding Religion in a Postmodern Context

This Chapter:
- Provides a psychology-based definition of postmodernism.
- Explains the biological limits of human understanding.
- Defines the concept of "bracketed absolute truths."
- Provides a definition of belief.

"The Gods Must Be Crazy" is the title of a movie from 1980. It is a story of an African tribesman who happens to be walking in his isolated part of the world when an airplane pilot high above throws an empty Coca Cola bottle out of the plane window. It lands close to the tribesman who has never seen such a thing: it is green but clear, and it has a shape that can hold water and make sounds when blown. It is hard. At first the tribesman believes this is sent from his god. But later, as he shares it with his tribe, it causes much angst, as individuals desire to possess the item. Jealousy and fighting ensue among the tribe's people until, with much dismay, the tribe begins to define the thing as evil. The tribesman, who was first blessed with what everyone thought was a god-sent gift, soon was faced with having to remove the item from the tribe and to journey to throw it off the edge of the earth (what most of us would understand as an ocean cliff). The movie is the story of his comical journey to the edge of the earth to dispose of the curse.

I learned about God's gifts as a good Roman Catholic boy growing up in Catholic schools and Sunday church services. The Roman Catholic Church played a large role in my life, as I fully embraced Catholic teachings in my youth. Daily I would attend mass with my fellow students. Mass was spoken in Latin then, and although most of us did not understand much in Latin, the ritual was mesmerizing, as we experienced deep tones of organ music reverberating through our souls with the thick smell of incense and candle wax. There stood a "priest," a holy man, in an ornate robe standing before an altar preparing to make a sacrifice. And we, the proud followers of the tradition, would line up to eat the flesh and drink the blood of Jesus—Jesus incarnate in the bread and wine. This ritual meant much to me at the time, as I experienced Jesus' presence at those moments when I joined my church community in worshiping his words and actions. Jesus was there among us and with us. I still feel this powerful emotion when I attend Roman Catholic Church services.

I suspect someone raised outside of the Christian tradition could observe what goes on in a Catholic church and view it as abhorrent. In fact, some members of organizations like "Jews for Jesus" or the Messianic Jews (Jews that believe Jesus was the Messiah), have argued that the Roman Catholic Church's traditions embody pagan rituals—a priest at an altar surrounded by fire making a sacrifice and then offering up flesh and blood to followers. Some have argued this is not in keeping with Jesus' Jewish heritage. They have a point. But to Catholics, little thought is given to the nature of their ritual—they have defined it as a holy offering. For them it is communion with Christ—getting Christ as close to one's soul as possible by consuming his body and blood.

Once the mass was allowed in English, it had even more meaning to me. I could witness the full sensory experience of the mass while hearing the words of my mentors saying, "This is the lamb of God who takes away the sins of the world. Happy are those who come to his supper." God and Jesus were defined as one with the Holy Spirit, a ghost floating around somewhere outside of us, but real and capable of influencing human events.

I believed in God as an omniscient and universal truth. Beyond feeling God's presence among my Christian brethren, I agreed with the idea that he was ever present—outside as well as inside of me, and outside and beyond common human experience. I have come to question my faith. I have come to a new understanding of religion.

Understanding Understanding: Defining the "Real"

When my son Christopher was a little guy, he and I decided to rent and to watch the movie Superman II (1980) starring Christopher Reeve. In the movie, Superman walks across the street distracted by an impending crisis, and while crossing the street he gets hit by a taxi cab. The taxi was destroyed by Superman's leg. As I watched the movie I looked over to my 3-year-old son, and I had a sinking feeling. I didn't want Christopher to think humans (or super humans) could walk into the path of an oncoming car and survive without a scratch. I paused the movie and took Chris to the garage where I showed him our car, and I had him hit the chrome bumper. "Hard," I said … "This will hurt you." "Danger! Cars are dangerous to people outside." Chris seemed to understand, and then I communicated, "Superman is pretend, Chris. He's not real. He's make-believe in the movies on TV." Again he seemed to understand. Well Christopher is now 27 years old and a father himself, so I guess he learned the lesson of the dangerous car. He certainly learned that Superman was pretend.

How is it that we learn? How is it that we come to know truths? In my youth, I believed we learned "facts" about what was "real" and "true." I always assumed that what I learned in school or in church was knowledge about what was objectively true. I have come to understand learning from a different perspective.

Language and Our Senses

There are few human words that are universal. The sounds associated with the word "mama" appear to be nearly universal, as you can question a person from a foreign culture and ask "How do you say 'mother' in your language?" It is a good guess that it will be an "mmm" sound. Also, the sounds of pain or loss (like the loss of a child) are universal—we recognize these sounds when we observe a mournful mother or father in real life or on television. There is no question about the expression of human suffering. But very few words can be viewed as universal. Humans are biologically wired to learn complex language, and they are capable of a large variation of language systems. In English, "internal" means inside, but in Italian, "intorno" means outside ("dentro" means inside). Eskimos have many words to describe snow (there are at least 10 words for snow in Inuit), but in my region of the United States, we just know if it is snow or sleet. So we are not hard-wired to learn one objective language or to understand things all the same way. One's way of understanding varies greatly by one's language, culture, and context. Our understanding through language is limited by the language itself, in other words.

Add to our bounded language the limitations of the human senses and the concept of "understanding" becomes even more constrained. Our sense organs are outstanding by comparison to other animals. We can see things in color with great depth perception. We can hear a wide array of sounds in our environment. We certainly can taste many varied flavors and textures. We are sensitive to feeling great pleasure or great pain. And of course, we know odors as varied as those of a bakery or those of a latrine. Biologically, our sensory system is rich. But it is not so rich as to allow perception of all that is "out there." For example, we only know if a dog whistle blows by the reaction of the dog; we certainly cannot hear at canine sound level or pitch. Canine sound perception is more acute than ours. We can assess this by devising a sensitive machine to amplify or otherwise to present the sound to us in a way we can perceive it. We can even make a machine that will allow the dog whistle sound to appear on a visual monitor. But without some sensory experience, it is unlikely we can understand anything we cannot perceive through some sensory means. There are sounds likely all around us all the time that we cannot perceive. Those sounds can only be understood by us if they are somehow made real through some sense perception.

My color blue may not be your color blue. Although there are common human physical structures of perception, any "true" understanding of what you see when you say "blue" versus what I see when I say "blue" is not possible. Our sensory system—our sense organs in relation to the rest of our nervous system—is a closed system (not thermodynamically closed, but closed to information). The only way we can come to agreement about the color blue, green, yellow, red, or any color, is to act in a coordinated fashion around the presentation of such a color. When we drive we all act as if red means stop, and that's a good thing, because if the meaning of the color "red" had not been taught and referenced in experience by drivers, we would have quite a traffic problem. Your red and my red may not be exactly the same, but the fact that we both learned "a red" in response to an electric signal has real meaning in the course of everyday driving events.

What we experience is very limited by our sense system and what we know or understand about our experiences is further limited by the language applied to those experiences.

What of the Souls on Mount Olympus?

When Zeus commands, no one listens. Zeus was one of the most influential and powerful gods of the ancient world. He was a patriarch—a grand master who oversaw Mount Olympus as a sometimes benevolent and sometimes malicious despot. On a whim he could punish or reward his followers. Even today there are some followers of the Greek gods, but the influence of those gods over the course of human events is limited. Without adherents, the rituals and beliefs that once guided a large percentage of the human race become meaningless. Zeus is not present in the lives of most individuals because they do not share beliefs with those who worship him. What of the souls on Mount Olympus? The souls on Mount Olympus have vanished with the followers of Zeus.

Can you name the three primary gods of Hinduism, the oldest extant large religion (the third largest religion on earth)? I've done a little survey, and most American Christians are unable to name Brahma, Vishnu, or Shiva as prominent Hindu deities. Yet Hinduism influences large numbers of people and the influence is pervasive in India and parts of the Middle East (and other parts of the world as well). Are Hindus in rural India to be faulted if they have never heard of Jesus Christ? It's incomprehensible to most Christians that people do not know or have not heard of Jesus Christ. Yet most Christians have no idea of Krishna's identity (he's thought to be an incarnation of Vishnu, and he is viewed as an avatar, or a messenger god).

I no longer believe in a universal god. I no longer believe that humans are capable of knowing with certainty a universal truth. I have come to realize that what we know is reflective of our biological limits within a social, linguistic, and cultural context. My working hypothesis is that we learn through relationships, just as my son Christopher learned about chrome bumpers and Superman. In other words, within the context and confines of our bodies and language systems, we come together to believe by sharing our understanding of our experiences. Belief is acting with others as if some socially defined concept represents truth. There is no mystery of faith—faith is people believing together.

Postmodernism

The judgment day has come, and the judgment is clear: ancient religions can no longer serve the needs of humanity. It is a sad thought for me to consider that today's prominent world religions carry a very heavy baggage. For example, Hinduism has a caste system that leaves many hopeless regarding their social status in their lifetimes; only through death and reincarnation can they move up in status. Buddhism is based on the very negative premise that life is suffering, which must be overcome. Also, I don't believe many Christians, Muslims, or Jews really acknowledge the very negative values at the foundation of their religions, such as sexism and degradation of women, prejudice against gays and lesbians, the association of physical and mental disability with sin, provincialism, anti-scientism, condemnation of large numbers of the human race who are viewed as non-believers, and evangelism at the cost of native traditions. These religions are fundamentally intolerant of difference, although on the surface most believers ignore or are unaware of these foundational values.

Postmodernism is an answer to these concerns. Postmodernism is an intellectual movement in the social and behavioral sciences, in literature, and in art. It is contrasted with "modernism," which I equate with concrete thinking. What is concrete is known unto itself—everything has objective characteristics which can be known in exactly the same way by all human beings. A block of concrete is a block of concrete, no matter who views it. That is modernism. Postmodernism is non-concrete. It allows for variation of understanding about what may be viewed as concrete. A concrete block can be viewed by some as a building block, but it can be viewed by others as a dinner table. The meaning of the thing we call a concrete block comes not from the nature of the block itself, but from the definition that humans give the block as they act around it. As another example, consider that a warrior is taught by superiors that a sharp blade is a weapon; however, a wood carving apprentice is taught that a sharp blade is a tool to create art. A vision of a sharp blade, therefore, has different meaning for the warrior and the wood carver. Postmodernism allows an infinite number of definitions around the experiences humans share.

What we sense and share with others is given meaning through interaction. But human interaction is limited by sense organs and the culture and traditions that are reflected in language. A butcher and a dairy farmer may understand the meaning of the word "cow" quite differently; and to a Hindu, a cow is sacred.

If we recognize that we cannot experience a "god" outside our sensory system, then what we define as godlike or sacred depends on our ability to share our sensory experiences with others and to come to agreement about the meaning of those experiences. Physiologically, what a Christian monk experiences in deep prayer may be very similar to what a Buddhist monk experiences in meditation, but the meaning of those experiences derives from the traditions and definitions their respective religions place on such experiences: a Christian monk may experience "God," and a Buddhist monk may experience "nirvana" or "enlightenment."

Postmodernism, then, is all about meaning. It is all about understanding. It's not about whether there is a sun in the sky, for example. But it is about how people define and understand the sun. The sun means something different to those who belong to a sun worshiping community than, for instance, an astronomer. Postmodernism allows for diverse understanding of human experiences. It allows for interpretation and narration around shared phenomena. It does not deal with concrete truth. It deals with "consensualized truth"—truth that comes from people sharing their most profound understanding of their experiences.

Bracketed Absolutes (Consensualities)

When I enter a Roman Catholic Church, I feel the presence of Jesus Christ. He is in the music, in the Gospel, in the physical symbols that adorn the church. I deeply experience his pain, as I view the statue of his body hanging from the cross. He suffered to show his unyielding faith in his god. I study his words from the Gospel reading and know at that moment that he is with me among the members of the congregation, fully as a presence. For me, as for many in the church I suspect, real meaning comes from weekly visits to church. I believe that Jesus' presence there among his adherents is an absolute. For the congregation, it is truth.

Although I was raised Roman Catholic, as a student of religion, I have come to know other traditions.

There are times when I am alone and I retreat to my backyard, to my patio, which is surrounded by a small wooded area. When I take a seated position and close my eyes, placing my hands on my knees palms up with my index fingers and thumbs touching lightly, I enter a feeling of deep relaxation. First, I see brown through my closed eyelids, and then pink as my eyes adjust to the penetrating light. I breathe slowly and visualize the image of Buddha, seated under the Bodhi Tree (the spot where he achieved enlightenment). I imagine my physical self dispersing in the wind, visualizing disintegration and oneness with my surroundings. I sense the sun penetrating my skin and I smell the scents of my surroundings. I feel my back and legs sinking slowly into the ground. And I taste the wind as I relax my jaw. At these moments of deep relaxation, I sense what Buddha may have sensed. He taught harmony with one's surroundings as he gave a lesson of oneness and selflessness. I feel his presence at those moments. His teachings are absolutely real to me as I follow his method and the teaching of those who followed in his footsteps.

I understand now what a Muslim must feel in ritual prayer

(Salah), prostrate and bowing in submission in the direction of Mecca. I know too that Hindus have a sense of self when surrounded by a deity and the active presence of those who have come before, reincarnate in them. I know now what a Jew might feel standing before the Wailing Wall. I understand now.

When people act in accord with the language and traditions represented in a religion, they find truth. The truth is made absolute by nature of the social and cultural landscape which embodies the tradition, as people interact around the teachings of spiritual guidance. Each truth, therefore, is made absolute through the interactions of people in their religious traditions. They embrace the truth of their religion. It is real to them. But what may be absolutely true to a Christian may not be absolutely true to a Jew. What may be real for a Buddhist may be far different for a Muslim. But each truth has validity within its group of adherents. This is the concept of "bracketed absolutes" [absolute], where truth is bounded by the interactions of people when communicating about the truth. Truth, therefore, comes from relationships.

Consider that the sensory experiences of mystics (whether one practices Judaic Kabbala, Islamic Sufism, or Hindu Vedanta) are probably very similar, but the interpretations of the experiences of the mystics comes from the languages that surround their religious actions. One does not purposefully follow a religious tradition to achieve a state of being outside of the tradition. To be outside of the tradition is to be outside of language, and outside of the human realm. Meaning comes especially from the teaching that preceded or accompanied an act, because it puts the experience in context. When language or symbolism is associated with an experience, there is meaning associated with the experience. Mystics practice with the intent of transcending language, but ironically their intent binds them to the human realm where all meaning is housed. Otherwise their actions would be meaningless. Where one seeks

16

"emptiness" one finds the fullness of language, as the concept of "emptiness" can only be distinguished in the social realm. So mystics are like good bakers—they follow a recipe to some end, and in doing so they find something very palatable.

What of visions? Are they not outside of language? The Virgin Mary does not appear to Hindus in rural eastern India. Most Christians, likewise, would not likely interpret a vision as Shiva or Vishnu. Few can understand that a vision is inside one's head, but any measurable meaning is outside one's head in the social matrix.

Social Validation and "Common Sense"

As my father was near death and without consciousness, he suddenly sat erect in his bed, opened his arms and reached forward, smiled, and then reclined. He, I am certain, had a vision, and a pleasant vision at that. Perhaps he saw my mother, his loving wife of over 50 years, who actually was with me sitting on the other side of the bed. Or perhaps he saw his parents or siblings. Perhaps he saw his god. I'll never know, except that I know his vision was real to him. He died one week later.

If you have any doubt about how real hallucinations feel to people hallucinating, visit a nursing home and walk the halls. There is much emotion attached to these experiences, as a person senses something others of us are unable to sense. Observing people talking to or even arguing with loved ones who are not there is a common occurrence. Of course, people see things that are not there too. The only way one can know that an experience is not a hallucination is for someone else to validate the experience as "real."

A few years ago I observed two people walking on the street in front of me; one stopped and turned suddenly looking around as if searching for someone. I heard her say to her friend, "Did you hear my name called?" Her friend said, "No." But she said, "I'm certain that I heard my named called!" Her friend responded with an abrupt, "Come on, you're hearing things!" I chuckled to myself, because I have had a similar experience. It sure seemed real at the time, but because the experience could not be socially validated ("common sense," or sensing in common with others), there is no way to know.

Knowledge is not something unto itself. Knowledge is in relationships. If a person, for example, is considering a religious vocation and hears his name called, and no one else hears, but a Christian friend explains, "That was the voice of God calling you," then that interpretation holds weight.

We go through life not knowing if what we experience is real or hallucination, except that the human nervous system is so rich that we can experience something and at the same time (or subsequently) talk about the experience. We can make love and call it "love" at the same time. Our ability to symbolically address that which we experience together is very powerful and unequaled in the animal world. It gives meaning to life. It brings our experience to an abstract level. No other animal has such a highly developed faculty.

As a psychologist I was taught that when people hallucinate multiple voices that they experience outside their heads, or when a hallucination is multi-sensory (e.g., both seeing and hearing), those are very serious diagnostic signs. Such hallucinations are associated with the most debilitating mental illnesses—those that cut people off from meaningful social interaction. When the ability to recognize a voice as reflecting a validation of shared experience is lost, then there is little hope of helping that person to live a socially meaningful life. Directly affecting the nervous system through medication becomes one of the only options to reconnect the person to the social world. With the elderly or seriously demented, such intervention may be less than useful.

Our nervous systems are closed, which becomes especially obvious when we observe a newborn baby (whose senses are undeveloped) or when our own senses begin to fail (as with the elderly). It is obvious that newborns and the very elderly operate on internal sensation. In old age as our senses fail we are closed off to the social realm, because we cannot hear well or cannot see well. While our senses are healthy, we can experience a wide range of phenomena and simultaneously share those experiences with others. Those experiences become true to us (as if they were objective) within the constraints of our neurology and social interaction. Otherwise we cannot know if what we experience is shared or specific to our own nervous system's activity (e.g., hallucination).

Knowable "truth" always comes from sharing experiences with others. Faith comes from sharing our most profound understanding of our experiences with others. Truth becomes known only within the brackets of social interaction.

Off the Scale

Postmodernism as reflected in the concept of bracketed absolute truths (competing truths) is a significantly different philosophy from those of the past. Philosophy has typically placed our understanding on a continuum—a straight line scale from one idea to an opposing idea. The "reality" scale typically runs from "objectivity" (there is a truth that everyone can know) to "subjectivity" (truth is specific to each individual's interpretation). One of the hardest ideas for people to accept is that postmodernism takes philosophy off of the continuum. A cognitive biologist, Humberto Maturana, developed a theory of understanding that by today's standard is postmodern. He called his position "objectivity in parentheses." Objectivity in parentheses is the idea that what is viewed as objectively true happens in the parentheses of social interaction. In other words, truth is bounded by the social group's language and traditions. Effectively, we have the concept of "objectivity in parentheses" in a triadic position with objectivity and subjectivity—it's not on the continuum. The following diagram shows objectivity in parentheses (O) in its place separate from the subjectivity "S" versus objectivity "O" continuum.

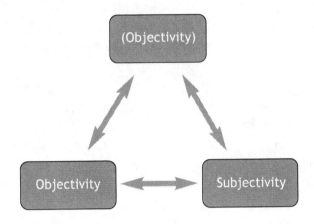

Postmodern philosophy is unique and not equated with either objectivity or subjectivity. Most people try to equate postmodernism with subjectivity, where anything goes or they equate it with "relativism." But postmodernism is a non-relative position that situates truth in relationships, rather than in one's head (subjectivity) or in the thing that is understood (objectivity). Relative truths are never absolute. But consensual truths are bracketed absolutes.

Escaping the objective-subjective continuum has important consequences. Facts cannot be known by individuals outside of their social context and language. Therefore, people can no longer make claims of individual conscience or self-determination, because "the mind becomes a form of social myth; the self-concept is removed from the head and placed within the sphere of social discourse" (Gergen, 1985, p. 271). There is no private language. Any conception of a "conscience" or a "self" grounds a person in the culture where the concept gets its meaning. The concept of free will and self-determination disappear into the social web. Rugged individualism, an American ideal, goes the way of the maverick. One cannot act individually outside of the sphere of one's heritage. One's heritage speaks clearly through one's words and actions.

How can one be a maverick when the concept itself is culturally loaded? A maverick can only emerge from a culture that distinguishes such behavior, and if it has been distinguished and defined, then it is part of the cultural landscape. All conceptualizations of individualism suffer the fate of the maverick—they become culturally embodied concepts. In American culture we are continually bombarded by such ideals, especially in the movies or television, whether it's the "Lone Ranger," Rooster Cogburn, Batman, Han Solo, or Indiana Jones, there's always the rogue who takes the lead contrary to advice or prevailing wisdom. The irony is that these heroes are lonely figures, and in the end, they play out the role to cliché. Closer examination reveals that these heroes are really steeped in tradition, as Batman was trained by Ninja renegades and the Lone Ranger has an influential but unassuming sidekick named Tonto.

We cannot act out of free will, unless by doing so we acknowledge we are embodying the cultural ideal of the individual independent decision maker. There is no autonomy; there is only accordance. There is no independence; there are only degrees of dependence. To survive without others and absent of shared language or symbolic interaction is to return to the animal world. True subjectivity is a non-human activity. It is akin to King Kong (as in the 2005 movie *King Kong*), where Kong, before he is taken from his island, has a quiet moment to view a sunset with Ann Darrow, but he is unable to share the meaning of his vision in meaningful interaction with his leading lady.

The concept of subjectivity is seductive but it has its limits (it makes one like King Kong). Objectivity also has its problems. Yet the idea of objectivity is an exciting alternative to subjectivity, and it is a philosophy that has guided us through the modern era.

Objectivity promotes concrete understanding of the world. It offers "the" answers. Where subjectivity provides the romantic individual ideal, objectivity raises the bar. Objectivity purports a high level truth—one that is elusive, but none-the-less, a knowable fact of nature. Objectivity says there are at least knowable organizing principles that got us here. This is what Einstein sought. He wanted to understand what was true. He felt there was an organizing ideal in the Universe—Spinoza's "god." And he felt that nature had truths that did not emerge out of probability. He wanted to know what was real. Ironically, he was the father of the theory of relativity, which defined space and time, mass and energy as relative concepts (not truths unto themselves). He was the master of relationships in physics.

Firmly press your index finger against a desk or table top (or any hard surface). Press hard enough to create some discomfort in your finger. Can you ever feel the surface? The answer is "no." What you actually feel is your nerve endings in the skin covering the tip of your finger against your bone. You can never feel the surface, you can only feel what is inside of you. If you do the exercise with someone else, though, you may actually come to agreement that what you feel is the table (or desk, or whatever other surface you say you encountered). We experience the world through our closed nervous system, which is activated at our boundaries. Our sense organs act as boundary markers. You can never escape those boundaries, except to hope that another human is near to stimulate your nervous system socially at the same time as you experience some "thing."

One way to view how humans function is to assume that driving the "human machine" is like flying an airplane by only using an instrument panel. Maturana made this case in an interview with Simon (1992; originally published in 1985). He indicated that humans function like a plane operating in the dark or in a deep fog. Nothing can be seen outside the windows.

The pilot can only be guided by the instrument panel, which for humans is their sensory (internal) experience. I would add that a pilot of the human machine also has a radio that connects to an outside (social) source that can define whether the pilot is "on course" (whether the instrument panel is working in a way others can verify). If the radio goes dead, all social validation ceases, and the pilot is fully dependent on the condition of the instrument panel. If it is operating accurately, the plane will land safe and sound. If it is inaccurate, there is real danger the plane will crash and burn. While operating the human machine, we have working radios and we need people communicating to us on our radios. It is the social realm that makes us fully functioning humans, because it takes at least two people to make something (defined) understood. This is the process I call "consensualizing."

There is a joke, the author of which is unknown to me, about an individual in a mental institution claiming to be Napoleon Bonaparte. His psychiatrist attempts to convince the individual that he is not Napoleon, and that he is living a delusion (a false conclusion about what is "real"). Frustrated with the patient's resistance and persistent claim that he was Napoleon, the psychiatrist yelled, "Well, who told you that you are Napoleon?" The patient yelled back, "God did!" At which point a voice was heard coming from the adjoining room responding, "I did not!"

Psychiatry is an interesting profession—as interesting as it is sad. Psychiatrists are often in the position of defining "truth" as objective in a world that is consensual. The 1994 *Diagnostic and Statistical Manual of Mental Disorders* now in its fourth edition, is a book that provides a taxonomy of mental disorders—a list of those "conditions" that constitute mental illness inside the person. It's an offshoot of the disease model of medicine, yet each categorical "disorder" is defined by a subgroup of "experts" who define the criteria for a diagnosis of a mental disorder. Few of the disorders actually are founded on evidence of biological or genetic correlation. Those disorders tend to be the most serious, such as schizophrenia, bipolar disorder (manic depressive illness), intellectual deficiency, alcoholism, and very severe depression. Most of the categories represent a compilation of signs, symptoms, and patterns of behavior that are viewed as typical of a condition. Literally, votes are taken about both the nature of a condition and its symptom pattern. Homosexuality, once thought to be a mental disorder, was removed from the third edition of the *Diagnostic and Statistical Manual of Mental Disorders*, not because the pattern of behavior changed, but for political and social justice reasons. The consensual truths that emerge from the debate over what conditions should be included in the *Diagnostic and Statistical Manual of Mental Disorders* are subsequently acted upon by mental health professionals as representative of real illness. But as Thomas Szasz, a psychiatrist and social theorist, explained in his book *The Myth of Mental Illness* (1960), psychiatrists are actually acting more like judges than medical doctors. Szasz's arguments were compelling, because he challenged the consensus of his colleagues in his own profession about the medical nature of their practices. He argued that psychiatry was really a societal control mechanism for addressing social deviance. His arguments, however, appear to have fallen on deaf ears, as little has changed in the manner in which psychiatry operates. This is an example of the power of consensual truths.

Consensualities Gone Awry

Some people believe there is danger in postmodernism, because it allows for an "anything goes" philosophy. Any group can come to agree on any "truth" no matter how harmful, hateful, or ridiculous it may sound to outsiders. But postmodernism does not make truths, it simply explains them.

On March 26, 1997, 39 people as part of a religion called

"Heaven's Gate" were awaiting anxiously for the arrival of the Hale-Bopp comet. They had, as a group, come to agreement that a spaceship followed the comet, and the spaceship would magically take them up and carry them to "the next level," a heaven of sorts. They committed mass suicide, apparently in the belief that their spirits would rise to the spaceship which would carry them to the next level and away from the earth, which was about to be recycled (cleared of humanity). The fact that they acted on this belief without apparent coercion demonstrates how powerful shared beliefs can be (when beliefs are made real through a community of active adherents). From the perspective of outsiders, this action was abhorrent and identified as the result of cult mentality and the influence of deranged leaders, Marshall Applewhite and Bonnie Nettles, who together came to agreement that they were chosen, as in the *Bible's* Book of Revelation (11:3). Regardless, people died based upon the hopes of attaining spiritual transformation, and for the members of the Heaven's Gate community, it was their destiny. How many people have died for religious causes? How many religions promise something better than lived experience in the afterlife? The ideals of heaven or paradise provide powerful images made real through the art, song, and narrative of a faith tradition.

To the degree that a faith tradition improves the human condition, I can agree that it has value for humanity. Unfortunately, belief systems and religious truths can be detrimental, deadly, and harmful from a larger global perspective. We are at a point in time where fanatical religious groups, holding claims to god-given truths, are fighting aggressively against those they define as "infidels" or non-believers. It is ironic, because these fanatical groups take on the characteristics of hate groups in the name of religion.

Hate groups, just like groups of aggressive religious fanatics, develop a set of principles around which members rally. Hate groups hold anger and prejudice towards others.

They act to discriminate or to destroy those that belong to the target group of their hatred. Hate groups often take part in rituals and have a pledge or creed that members recite. Truth derives from their consensualizing, as they define an "enemy" or target of their enmity. Members of these groups will risk their own lives to carry out acts of hatred. Yes, consensualizing can go awry.

Postmodernism does not justify or excuse such actions, but it does explain how people come to believe the things that they do.

What makes a consensual truth valuable from a global perspective? How can we counter the power of consensualities that purport hatred or harm to others? The answer is: social agreement and commitment to consensually defined ethics.

Chapter Conclusion

This chapter has made the case that understanding comes from relationships. Biologically we experience the world through our sensory system, which is closed to information, except through stimulating the nervous system simultaneously through social interaction. Meaning derives from our ability to abstract and to experience our world in symbolic ways. We in effect socially construct our understanding of our world, including understanding of profound religious experiences. Truth, therefore, does not come from objective fact, and neither does it come from inside of a person; rather truth comes from consensualizing — deriving meaning of experiences through interaction with others.

What Does it Mean that a Human Nervous System is Closed?
A Dialogue
A student of postmodern religion addresses her teacher:

Student: "I'm having difficulty understanding the idea that our nervous systems are closed to information. I experience that I am open to new learning. How can one both be closed and open at the same time?"

Teacher: "There is a 'truth claim' in postmodern thought about how humans physiologically operate. It is an assumption with which postmodernists agree—a tenet of postmodern philosophy. It is one possible assumption among many other assumptions about how humans are physically organized and operate. That claim is that the neurological system of humans is a closed circuit of sorts."

Student: "But this truth claim, that humans biologically have closed nervous systems, makes no sense."

Teacher: "The claim is that humans are neurologically closed. That means that we cannot gain knowledge by direct contact with an outside world. This position holds that what we experience is nervous system activity. Our nervous systems are activated by interaction and then our perception is given meaning through simultaneous activation of the nervous system by symbolic interaction with other perceived humans. Those perceived other humans help us to interpret our experiences. Information is transmitted not from an external thing, but within the confines of our nervous system activity that is simultaneously perturbed perceptually and socially. That is what is meant by our nervous systems being 'closed.' When you feel, you feel your nerve endings in your fingers. When you see, the image is on your retina. When you hear, you hear the activity of your inner ear mechanism. We can learn, but only through interaction with others about those things we perceive using a shared (symbolic) language system. Our closed nervous systems are extended and expanded by symbolic communication. Maturana called this the 'consensual domain.'"

Student: "So how do I know the other people I experience are really there?"

Teacher: "They are real to you always, but another person may observe that the people you relate to are not observable.

That person would observe you as hallucinating. Most of the time we can tell if we are hallucinating, because hallucinations are infrequently multi-sensory, meaning you don't both hear and see a person at the same time in a hallucination. Usually people who are psychotic just hear voices. But, when a person acts as if someone is viewable and can be heard, that's pretty serious. If another observer is around, like a psychiatrist, that hallucinating person will probably be classified as "psychotic" or "demented."

Student: "So everything we experience can be hallucination?"

Teacher: "Yes. For some people it is, and, therefore, their survival is threatened. When the nervous system is closed to meaningful social interaction, as happens in very old age with the demented or with the very seriously ill, the person's existence is at risk. If our nervous systems are active in a way that actions cannot be validated by others, we perish. It would be like an electrical heating circuit in a home, where no one was available to adjust the thermostat, and the furnace burned itself out. The way we know the human machine is working correctly is if it survives. For most of us, perceived interaction leads to continued survival. As fully functioning humans, we operate well within a matrix of relationships and we survive through interaction. Our nervous systems may be closed, but we can find meaning in co-action with others to achieve defined goals and to survive. It is like walking through life with a blindfold while being directed by a guiding voice. If the voice is trustworthy, we can follow instructions and do just fine. If the voice disappears or if it is not trustworthy, we can easily be faced with danger. When we talk about "trustworthiness" we are talking about faith, which is where belief comes into play. Belief is acting with others as if some socially defined concept represents truth."

Student: "It is still a bit confusing, but I think I am beginning to understand."

Teacher: "Just remember this. The postmodern assumption about the human 'machine' is as follows: humans are wired to consensualize as a way to understand their world. We don't experience an objective world. We experience a world only as we can (neurologically) experience it and in relation to others."

Student: "That helps a little. Thank you, Teacher."

Chapter Two

Relationships are Everything, and Everything is Relationship

This Chapter:
- Argues that traditional theories of psychology have downplayed the influence of relationships on behavior.
- Purports that postmodernism requires a total shift to a relationship worldview.
- Describes how religion comes from relationships.

Sometimes I do not realize that postmodern philosophy is viewed by others as very radical. Often when I first try to explain these ideas to others (with little or no acquaintance with these ideas), their reaction is initially skepticism or disbelief. Later, after further interaction on these matters, these same skeptics begin to recognize that these ideas have some credibility.

As a student of psychology, I originally found postmodern ideas difficult to accept. I was a skeptic. In psychology, as I was taught, the focus of study is the individual—the isolated person. I was indoctrinated with classic personality theories, like those of Freud and Jung, and I was taught about behaviorism through the works of Watson and Skinner, as examples. I also learned theories of psychotherapy that focused on counseling individuals (alone as clients) about their problems. In all of these studies, the behavior or personality of an individual was examined with the influence of outside interpersonal interaction held somewhat constant, which is counter to postmodern ideas.

I know that not all readers will have acquaintance with psychological theories, but I feel it is important to review classic psychological ideas from a postmodern perspective. I will briefly review a few theories in psychology and will then add a comment or two that shows how the theorists ignored or downplayed interpersonal interaction. Because my journey to postmodernism took a path through psychology, it is the best way I know to provide you, the reader, with a similar framework for understanding the postmodern revolution.

The intent of this chapter is to make three points which are foundational to the application of postmodern philosophy to religion. First, relationships are everything (meaning that inter-action, and not objects or things, is the "stuff" of the universe). Second, everything is relationship (meaning that every perceived object can be redefined as a set of relationships). Third, healthy, loving, positive relationships are crucial to mental health and well-being.

Please bear with me as I attempt to help you understand (or better understand) a fully relational worldview. This relational viewpoint will lay the groundwork for a postmodern philosophy of religion.

The Realization

I believe that people do not exist as separate beings. I no longer believe in the concept of individuality. Though I am a psychol-ogist, I have totally rejected the psychology of the individual. It has been a long journey, and I feel obliged to explain how I arrived where I am. This realization has had a major effect on my understanding of both psychology and religion. The change to a relational worldview is the equivalent of switching perspec-tives between *mutually exclusive* worldviews. One cannot see people and relationships at the same time. It is like looking at a diagram where one's focus changes the perception significantly, and one cannot focus in two places (or two ways) at once. Consider the diagram of a vase, which follows. If you look closely at the vase, you will be attentive to the middle of the diagram. But if you allow your focus to travel to one side, you will see the outline of a man's face. In fact, there are two twin faces looking at each other in the diagram. So what do you see? The vase? Or two twins? Your perception will not allow you to see both the vase and the twins at the same time—the views are mutually exclusive.

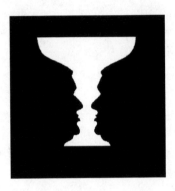

So too, postmodern philosophy is mutually exclusive to the psychology of the individual. Postmodern philosophy focuses our attention to relationships—the stuff between what we observe as things. Postmodernism is in the middle, like the vase. Classic psychological theory focuses on the individuals—each twin—trying to define traits and characteristics of each person (e.g., personality, intelligence, predispositions) or the factors that influence each person's behavior. Postmodernism directs us to look for the relational interpretation of that which we experience.

So here is a brief summary of the history of psychology in this regard. I will summarize a few of the most important developments in the history of psychology and counseling, and then I will describe how postmodern theory leads to a near total revision of thinking about how humans operate.

Classic Psychological Theory with a Twist

Psychology started with Freud's ideas that we have a "psyche," a non-physical structure that reflects one's personality. You cannot simply open a person's skull and find his or her psyche. It is a mental structure, an invisible "thing," with parts—a conscious (awareness), an unconscious (the stuff of the mind that only surfaces when one sleeps or when one is in a hypnotic trance, as examples), and a pre-conscious (a place where, with effort, we can retrieve information—it's the place where old phone numbers and addresses go that requires concerted effort to retrieve them). Freud viewed problems as inside one's head. Although relationships could affect an individual by helping the person develop a "moral conscience" designed to balance the inherited sexual and aggressive instincts, people inherited an "ego" to keep control of the inevitable conflicts between the social conscience and the biological drives. The ego is the mediator or go-between that is the psyche's means of keeping things in check. It's like the cartoonesque image of a head when there's a little devil on one shoulder and a little angel on the other trying to convince the head how to tell the body to act. Without a moral conscience the personality would run wild and humans would rape and pillage for the fun of it. On the other hand, an over constraining moral conscience produces a personality that is so out of touch with its inner drives, that even normal and safe biological impulses are suppressed. So humans have to be kept in balance, and the psyche has a mechanism of balance control. The "ego" is that mechanism—it is the personality's decision maker of sorts. A weak ego could lead to "neurosis," a term that Freud used to mean psychological disturbance where there was still contact with reality at some level, because wise decisions were being displaced by an over controlling moral conscience. "Psychosis" was the term used when the ego was so weak that only serious biological drives toward sex and destruction prevailed. The conflict between biological drives and social conscience runs rampant in one's psyche, with the unconscious being the hiding place for all that is socially unacceptable, even in children. Children were viewed by Freud as having unconscious inherited drives toward sex and aggression which emerge, according to Freud, in psychological complexes — such as the electra complex (little girls have sexual feelings for their fathers) and the oedipal complex (little boys have sexual feelings for their mothers).

As Freud developed his theory, at one point he entertained a very insightful hypothesis about childhood development. It was called the "seduction theory" (sometimes called the "seduction hypothesis"). The seduction theory stated that children were not just unconsciously fantasizing sexual feelings, they really were being seduced by adults. He theorized that such seduction was very destructive to their mental functioning. Freud probably, for whatever reason, considered this idea unacceptable. In fact he wrote a letter to a friend stating, "surely such widespread perversions against children are not very probable." Freud rejected the seduction theory, and instead developed his theory around childhood fantasy. He proposed that children were not really seduced by adults; they just unconsciously fantasized such seduction. Accordingly, they needed therapy to learn to manage these unconscious issues, such as sexual feelings. By today's standards, Freud made a huge mistake, because we know that child sexual abuse is pervasive across all cultures and societies and there is no fantasy or unconscious process at work — it is real adults taking advantage and abusing children. There are children who have been seriously abused by their caregivers with significant social and emotional consequences. I think most would agree, if there is evil in this world, this is a case of pure evil. And there's no devil involved — there are real adult perpetrators acting in ways that seriously harm others. Today, psychology has advanced to the degree we can explain such behavior, although we should never excuse it.

While Freud's place in the history of psychology is well secured, from my point of view, his rejection of the seduction theory was a grave error and set psychology on its first flight in the wrong direction. But Freud must be credited none-the-less with developing the first theory proposing mental health consequences from disturbed interpersonal interaction. In fact, some of his students took up the seduction theory and later developed a branch of Freudian theory that accepted seduction theory. That branch is called the "object relations school." The object relations school recognizes the powerful influence of early interpersonal relationships (objects from the past) on forming the personality.

About 20 years after Freud published his first major works (*The Interpretation of Dreams* and *The Psychopathology of Everyday Life*), John B. Watson began to apply ideas that humans were controlled more by external factors than internal conflicts. He applied Pavlov's idea (from experiments with dogs) to show that fear could be programmed into a child by associating something scary with something not so scary, until the not scary item became scary too. His first attempt worked; he conditioned a child (Little Albert) to fear a cute little white furry mouse by associating the presence of the animal with a loud frightening noise (always scary to a child). Watson, known as the "Father of Behaviorism," showed that people learn fears not from conflicts inside the personality, but from factors in the environment impinging the person.

In the mid-1900's B. F. Skinner took up the behaviorism banner where Watson left off. He developed a theory of operant (behavioral) conditioning and focused on what happens after a behavior rather than what comes before a behavior (as Watson had done). Skinner, following an idea first developed by Thorndike (the Law of Effect), decided to analyze in depth how animals react to reward and punishment. He found a very powerful link between what happens after a behavior and the likelihood the behavior will occur again. He learned that positive reinforcement (reward) was the best way to increase the likelihood of a behavior recurring. And he found that punishment, although the quickest and most efficient way to stop a behavior, had very serious negative consequences—increased aggressiveness and confusion (because the animal is not instructed by punishment how to act). Skinner proposed that human behavior could be best affected by rewards (to increase desirable behavior) and removal of rewards (to decrease undesirable behavior that is somehow being maintained by reinforcement). In either case, behavior of an individual is affected by outside factors (rewards) that are typically linked to basic needs, such as food, water, safety, and comfort.

Just as Freud did, Watson and Skinner either downplayed or ignored the relational aspects of their models. In the 1970's a humorous comic circulated in academic circles. It was a picture of a rat in a "Skinner box," an apparatus used to modify a rat's behavior by presenting food pellet rewards when the rat emitted behaviors wanted by the apparatus operator. The cartoon had the rat in the Skinner box talking to another rat friend in a nearby cage saying, "Yeah, I got this guy trained. Every time I press this lever, he gives me a treat!" The fact that somebody is standing around rewarding behavior speaks volumes about the relational aspects of reward. Reward doesn't come from thin air. Reward for humans typically comes from other humans—it comes through relationships. The person rewarding behavior is operating within some social context that defines control or modification of behavior as "valuable." That context cannot be ignored. The effort to control or to modify behavior places behavioral psychology in the social realm. Schools are a classic example. The burden of behavioral modification of children resides with parents first, but schools are often in the position of having to "socialize" misbehaving children—those that cannot collaborate well with others and those who cannot focus on the task of developing social responsibility and valuable skills for society. Behavioral control reflects the need for humans to cooperate, to collaborate, and to behave in a socially responsible manner in order to achieve goals. This is how humans have survived and thrived. Controlling or modifying behavior always results in a social outcome. Rewards (and punishments) are a means of socializing behavior, and they occur typically in the context of relationships at the interpersonal, societal, and cultural levels (and certainly in schools).

Psychology, as a discipline, has tended to ignore the big picture. Psychology is reductionistic in its focus, at the expense of understanding behavior from the larger perspective. Yet psychology has been very helpful in providing many small pieces to a big puzzle.

Overall, psychology has traditionally focused on the person, whether one views problems as coming from within or outside the person. The individual was the focus of a psychologist's observations and interventions. Psychologists, depending on their orientation, either looked for problems inside a person's mind, or they looked for factors outside the person that were impinging the person and affecting functioning. They tended to isolate the individual and not to view people within the context of healthy or unhealthy relationships.

It wasn't until the 1950's that theorists began to view inter-personal relationships as a major focus of study and as culprits in "mental illness." Gregory Bateson, a social theorist who was married to Margaret Mead (the famous anthropologist), became an advocate of a relational view of mental health. He and his colleagues observed the interaction between disturbed children (diagnosed as schizophrenic) and their mothers, and they defined the interaction as defective. They identified a pattern of interaction they called the "double bind," which is a no-win situation within the context of relationships. They proposed that a double bind could drive someone crazy.

As an example, imagine a pet owner with a misbehaving dog. Assume the pet owner is not very smart about human-pet relations. So when the pet runs away, the owner puts a doggie biscuit in one hand and a rolled up newspaper in the other.

When the dog approaches after being called by the owner, the owner gives the dog the biscuit at the same time he smacks him hard with the rolled up newspaper. In this case, the owner believes that he is rewarding the dog for returning and punishing the dog for running away. After this same scenario is carried out several times, the animal starts to shiver and shake when he approaches the owner after being called, and he begins to urinate on the owner's carpet every time he gets near. The dog is in a double bind and "can't win to lose" in this circumstance. Weird behavior then emerges. And in time, just the presence of the owner will create odd behavior.

That is what Bateson hypothesized: people will act strangely if put in double binds.

Bateson made a compelling argument for a social understanding of mental health problems, and many consider him to be a founder of "Social Systems Theory," a complex theory that purports that relationships are what primarily affect human behavior. Mental health professionals who subscribe to this model are much more likely to view problems within families or marriages rather than in or around a person in isolation. They are more likely to do marriage, couples, or family therapy.

Psychological theory has advanced so that practicing psychology now requires looking at internal and external factors affecting an individual. Practicing psychology also requires an astute psychologist or counselor to analyze relationships as they influence a person's emotional functioning.

This brief summary of psychology is rather unfair to the myriad of theorists and researchers who have contributed to the history of the discipline. Many people have contributed to our understanding of human behavior, and their contributions cannot be overstated. But hopefully, the preceding information provides an historical context for what I am about to propose. The question is, "How does all this talk about psychology relate to religion?" Here's how.

Going to the Extreme Against Buddha's Advice

Buddhism recommends a middle path (or middle way), avoiding extremes. The middle path ideal is thought to come directly from Buddha, and it is presented most clearly in the Pali Canon of Theravada Buddhism. Apologies to Buddha, because postmodernism has taken our understanding of human functioning to a relational extreme. Postmodern theory allows for a fully relational understanding of behavior. It also proposes a fully relational understanding of itself. Postmodernism puts all understanding of behavior in social contexts. It purports that everything we know comes from relationships. Beyond implications for psychology and the other mental health professions, it has major implications for our understanding of religion.

I have completely made the switch from viewing individuals and their concerns from the perspective of the psychology of the individual to viewing them as relational. I no longer see people (as odd as that may sound). When I look at someone, I see the embodiment of his or her parents' biological relationship. I see all of his or her social relationships reflected in dress, language, dialect, grammar, attitudes, and behavior. I see people as extensions of their biological and social networks. I view people as perceptual phenomena for the transmission of relationships. I see right through people (not literally) to the social and biological webs that connect them in the present and the past. And I see them with all of my relationships affecting my vision. The switch has gone off. There is no going back for me. I have been affected by the postmodern tidal wave—by my relationships to the postmodern theorists and by my family history and the values that resonate about the importance of social connection.

I no longer view religion out of context. I see Jesus with his disciples embracing the ideals of the Jewish prophets. I visualize Buddha with his students arising from the traditions that came before. I imagine Muhammad with his people standing strong against aggression in the harsh environment of the Middle East. I imagine the Jewish prophets relaying their ideals to a struggling populace under rule. I see a Hindu guide communicating the message of Krishna to those who will listen. I imagine all of this because I have come to understand the position that relationships are everything.

Religion is in language, and language is in relationships. Relationships are communication—by all means at all levels—verbal and symbolic, non-verbal, and contextual. When we communicate with others, we enter relationships with them. What makes us "the human species" revolves around our ability to communicate and to enter meaningful relationships. Religion is all about people engaging in meaningful relationships.

Past religious leaders knew this. That is why the religious leaders of the surviving religions made a serious effort to preserve their religious texts. They treated those documents with great care. They knew that without the written word communicating the religion's doctrine, the chances of the religion's survival were very low. In ancient times it was hard to communicate ideas orally in a way that could reach large numbers of people. But once mass means of communication developed, the written word became very important to education of the populace.

Would Christianity be known if there was no *Bible*? Would Islam be understood in the absence of the *Koran*? Would Buddhism be known if the students of Buddha did not write down his ideas (e.g., the *Dhammapada*)? Would we know Hindu thought in the absence of the Hindu texts (e.g., *Upanishads*; the *Bhagavad Gita*)? Why did the Jewish people make an effort to write their oral history and oral law (the *Talmud*)? Without the written word, or without the word communicated to large audiences, it is the postmodern premise that these religions would have been relegated to the likes of the ancient Greek and Roman religions—mythology. Christianity, Islam, Hinduism,

Buddhism, and Judaism all are known because they exist in relationships around which there is much communication at many levels. For a religion to survive, there must be a messenger, and there must be a well known message that others embrace and share. The message must be transmitted clearly and through the generations. It has to be an enduring message — one that is believable. And it has to be viewed as valuable to one's survival or to the survival of a way of life that one finds defensible within one's social order. Christ, Muhammad, the Hindu gods, Buddha, and the Jewish prophets live on through their words. They are with their adherents at those moments that the adherents intimately share the words and ideals communicated by their spiritual leaders. The spiritual guides live through their messages.

The postmodern implication is clear for those who believe in a god or who feel they must believe in a god. Their god is with them when they are in the language of their god. Their god is with them when they are among others of the same persuasion. They embrace their god as they embrace each other. Their god is with them, between them, and among them. Embracing their god is not a casual process, because their god is real to them — absolutely real — as they share the message with others or recite the words their god has communicated to them. Their god represents absolute truth within the context of those relationships. We honor and understand this from the postmodern perspective.

For those that have no faith in god, or who value science over religion, the postmodern ideal has much to offer. It offers a place where ideas like atheism, agnosticism, and scientism all have value. It offers a place aside the traditional religions where the study of that which has historically been understood as non-religious may take place. All forms of belief are honored by postmodernism, even those that purport a belief that no god exists.

However, beliefs that challenge the value of relationships, or that purport harm to others on some grounds, cannot be honored. The postmodern ideal is built upon the importance of relationships in human functioning. It is built on the assumption that relationships have value and that collaboration and cooperation are worthwhile. Ethical standards that define the merit of human relationships are crucial to the postmodern message. Without ethical standards that communicate a message of the value of human relations, the voices of hate, discrimination, arrogance, selfishness and prejudice will have equal volume to the voices of collaboration, cooperation, and co-action for the betterment of humankind.

Chapter Conclusion

Whereas classic psychological theory focuses on individualism, postmodernism focuses on relationships. Psychology may be re-conceptualized by means of a relational worldview—a view that is mutually exclusive to the psychology of the individual. Human behavior is understood as interactive when viewed through the postmodern lens. And religion, too, involves relationships. Outside of relationships, religion has no meaning or influence on human events. The role of religion in the postmodern era must be to model the ideal of healthy and beneficial relationships, which are crucial to mental health. Relationships are everything, and religion is relationships. Ideally, ethical rules for interaction will be accepted and followed to ensure that religion will lead to the betterment of humankind.

Trying to Understand that Everything is Relationship:
A Dialogue
A student of postmodern religion addresses her teacher:

Student: "I'm not understanding the idea that everything is

42

relationships. That seems ridiculous, because I see 'things.'"

Teacher: "This is one of the hardest ideas for students of postmodernism to grasp. Remember, what you see is not 'out there.' It is in relation to your nervous system. When you see some 'thing,' it is really an impression on your retina. So you really see the 'thing' only as you can see it—it is in relationship to you. We define the external world only through internal processes in relationships to other human beings."

Student: "But it is still hard to deny that some 'thing' that we see is out there."

Teacher: "The only way we can know it is 'out there' is for others to validate that they observe something they describe in words similar to your own description of the 'thing.' This assumes that you have a language in common with others."

Student: "Okay, so we actually perceive things in relationship to ourselves and to other human beings. I can get that. But isn't what we observe still a 'thing?'"

Teacher: "From a postmodern perspective, all things are redefined as relationships. It is just assumed that it is easier for us to see things rather than the complex of relationships that is their nature. I am my mother's and my father's biological relationship; their relationship lives through me. I appear to you to be a 'thing,' but I am a relationship between two genetic pools of relationships. When you look at me you are seeing my parents' relationship."

Student: "I never looked at you like that."

Teacher: "Postmodern thinkers see all things as the relationships that compose them. So things really become perceptual phenomena for the transmission of relationship. All my biological and social relationships speak through me. I am a sort of conduit for relationships."

Student: "So you are some sort of means for relationships to manifest themselves?"

Teacher: "Postmodernism teaches us to view all things as

means for relationships to manifest themselves, and they are observed and identified only in relationships to our nervous system and through social validation."

Student: "That is a really different way of looking at the world."

Teacher: "Yes, once one defines things as relationships, one has made a switch to a postmodern philosophy."

Student: "I will struggle with this, because I have been taught that things exist as objects which have traits and qualities."

Teacher: "That is your indoctrination in modernist thought speaking through you. The more you interact with postmodern thinkers on these matters, the easier it will become for you to understand postmodern philosophy and to apply it to religion."

Student: "Thank you, Teacher."

Chapter Three

Ethics

This Chapter:
- Redefines the idea of "survival of the fittest" for humans to mean good fit within a thriving social group of affiliation.
- Argues that ethics, the standards we live by, have been largely communicated through religion.
- Provides a definition of the "human spirit."
- Proposes that postmodernism provides a framework for defining some possible ideals for orderly living.

When I use the term "ethics," I use it in the casual sense, not as used in the discipline of philosophy where the study of ethics addresses theories of right and wrong. I use it to mean, rather, general standards or principles of action. Therefore, ethics in this book will mean general guidelines of behavior.

The term ethics as I use it here actually may mean what a true philosopher would call "morals." Unfortunately, the term "morals" has come to be associated with specific religious views or dogma, an association which I am trying to avoid. When I think of ethics, I try to consider concepts or ideals that cross cultures and religions and that guide large numbers of people. For me, defining ethics means searching for behavioral constructs that can be associated with improvement of the human condition—concepts that are associated with advancement, collaboration, and the fulfillment of human basic and social needs.

I do not believe humans have survived as a species because humans are adept at physically adapting to the environment. For example, we don't have much of a "coat" so-to-speak, as our skin is very fragile and sensitive. Other animals have thicker, stronger, and more adaptable natural coverings. Dogs, for example, have heavy coats in the winter, but shed in the summer. Consider an alligator—there's a creature with some tough skin. What humans have that makes them unique and so adaptable is a rich nervous system, headed by a brain with billions of nerve cells that intertwine and intermix in very complex ways. We have evolved into something very special.

Our rich nervous system has benefits. It allows us to share experiences both through our sense organs and by talking to each other at the same time. For example, we can look at something with someone else and simultaneously communicate about what we see. The human brain is so complex and rich that different parts of it can be stimulated and active at the same time through different senses (seeing and hearing, for example). In other words, complex actions can be coordinated both by the senses and by intricate symbolic communication through sound or other means. This makes it easy, for example, for humans to hunt together or to work together to build shelter or forage for food.

Human infants are totally helpless and must be nurtured and protected. A baby can survive only though collaboration of parental partners or a social support system. Unlike other species where offspring at birth can survive essentially alone, human babies take a long time to mature. It takes many years of maturing to reach independence from parents, and as some parents will tell you, it takes longer for their children to mature than they expected. It also takes more than two hands to raise a child. Childrearing not only depends on maternal instinct, but it happens best in a system of support. Our prehistoric ancestors learned to survive in groups, because group effort provided a measure of security and a method for successful childrearing, hunting, and food gathering. We survive because we work well together.

We work together. We collaborate. We are a species that can share loving attention and define it as worthwhile. We can be aggressive when threatened, but we do best when we find ways to co-exist peacefully in communities of shared responsibility. We value life and will act especially to protect our offspring. We need our basic needs met for safety, food and shelter. So we appreciate a territory that can help to sustain us. But we must respect the boundaries of others' territories, or there may be retribution and a threat to livelihood. We have learned to defend a territory necessary for survival.

Because our nervous systems are so rich, we have also come to share and to appreciate art. Visually we recognize beauty. We find pleasure in a variety of sounds and rhythms. We enjoy narratives—stories that help to give meaning to life, and we especially enjoy the freedom to express ourselves through our art and stories. We have learned not only to address our world on concrete terms, but we have learned that we are capable of abstraction—dealing with intangibles both to address and to understand our nature and our environment.

Through civilization we have advanced beyond what ancestors could have imagined. Leonardo da Vinci or Benjamin Franklin would be amazed. Today, I can walk into a super-market opening doors with the wave of a hand like a Jedi Knight. I can communicate with my son while he is visiting his in-laws halfway around the world using a small wireless device in the palm of my hand. I can welcome strangers from far away lands into my house by pushing a button on a flat screen to gain a visual picture of them and to hear their voices as my children play nearby. We are unique among the animal species.

We have learned to live a civilized way by means of rules of interaction. We have developed, for example, laws for orderly living. We have established methods of enforcement, which we empower through established government. We have learned to live in crowded environments by standards that direct organized and cooperative interaction. Our inbred instincts to collaborate are powerful and have prevented full expression of our aggressive instincts.

By living by a code, we thrive. But what code? Who defines the rules of engagement? Who gets credit for the code we thrive by? Our gods do.

God Told Me

Scholars believe that the Hindu text entitled the Bhagavad Gita ("The Song of the Blessed One") was written some time between the fifth century before the Common Era and the first century before the Common Era. Written in poetic form, it tells the story of two clans of a warring family from India. Two armies were on the verge of battle. The leader of one army is the virtuous Arjuna, the hero of the story. Opposing Arjuna and his army is the army of Kauravas, the evil cousins. As the armies assemble at opposite ends of a battlefield and are about to engage in war, a charioteer named "Krishna" drives Arjuna to the center of the battlefield where Arjuna can survey the scene. Krishna turns out to be a god incarnate, the incarnation of the god Vishnu and an avatar (or messenger). Positioned between two armies poised for battle, time suddenly slows and all that is around Arjuna is likened to stillness. Krishna begins, at that moment, to teach Arjuna lessons about love, life, eternity, reincarnation, the self, and the need to defend against unprovoked aggression. No where can these lessons have more meaning than at a moment in time and space where one is about to face likely death in the name of a cause. It is both surreal and compelling. Krishna speaks:

> The self who dwells in the body
> is inviolable, forever;
> therefore you have no cause to grieve
> for any being, Arjuna.

Know what your duty is
and do it without hesitation.
For a warrior, there is nothing better
than a battle that duty enjoins.

Blessed are warriors who are given
the chance of a battle like this,
which calls them to do what is right
and opens the gates of heaven.

Krishna continued:

In order to protect the good,
to destroy the doers of evil,
to ensure the triumph of righteousness,
in every age I am born.

Whoever knows, profoundly,
my divine presence on earth
is not reborn when he leaves
the body, but comes to me.

Released from greed, fear, anger,
absorbed in me and made pure
by the practice of wisdom, many
have attained my own state of being.

However men try to reach me,
I return their love with my love;
whatever path they may travel,
it leads to me in the end.

And to make it clear that he, Krishna, was a credible source, he
revealed himself as a divine vision to Arjuna:

After he had spoken these words,
Krishna, the great Lord of Yoga,
revealed to Arjuna his majestic,
transcendent, limitless form.

With innumerable mouths and eyes,
faces too marvelous to stare at,
dazzling ornaments, innumerable
weapons uplifting, flaming—

crowned with fire, wrapped
in pure light, with celestial fragrance,
he stood forth as the infinite
God, composed of all wonders.

If a thousands suns were to rise
and stand in the noon sky, blazing,
such brilliance would be like the fierce
brilliance of that mighty Self.

Arjuna saw the whole universe
enfolded, with its countless billions
of life-forms, gathered together
in the body of the God of gods.

Through this poem not only is a god revealed, but his doctrine is espoused. The poem continues with lessons about the need to be courageous in self-defense, to do one's best and relinquish attachment, to understand that life is eternal as the soul is passed from generation to generation, and to find a way to heaven through love, benevolence, and peace.

The Bhagavad Gita is an epic and an ethic. It is a lesson to mere mortals. It provides rules to live by.

A god not only has spoken to Arjuna, but a god has also

spoken to Moses. In the Book of Exodus, God made it known to Moses that the Israelites had to live by his law and not honor false gods. He provided Moses with a list of Commandments, from God himself and written in stone, so that Moses could make known God's wishes to his people. Unfortunately, while Moses was on Mount Sinai receiving the message from God, his people betrayed God and began to worship a golden calf. God became angry, but Moses sought forgiveness for his people. God was unforgiving and "sent a plague upon the people for what they did with the calf that Aaron made" (*Torah*, Exodus 32). The "Ten Commandments" were God's law, and to fail to follow them could bring on the wrath of God. The *Torah* (Exodus 20) states:

> I, the Lord, am your God, who brought you out of the land of Egypt, the house of bondage: You shall have no other gods besides Me. You shall not make for yourself a sculptured image, or any likeness of what is in the heavens above, or on the earth below, or in the waters under the earth. You shall not bow to them or serve them. For I the Lord your God am an impassioned God, visiting the guilt of the parents upon the children, upon the third and upon the fourth generations of those who reject Me; but showing kindness to the thousandth generation of those who love Me and keep my commandments.

And other commandments followed:

> You shall not swear falsely by the name of the Lord your God; for the Lord will not clear one who swears falsely by His name.
> Remember the Sabbath day and keep it Holy. ...
> Honor your father and your mother, ...
> You shall not murder.

You shall not commit adultery.

You shall not steal.

You shall not bear false witness against your neighbor.

You shall not covet your neighbor's house:

You shall not covet your neighbor's wife, nor his male or female slave, nor his ox or ass, nor anything that is your neighbors.

And so, the Jewish people were given rules to live by. They were god-given rules, and failure to follow the rules had dire consequences.

For Christians, there is one added commandment. Jesus taught his followers to love one another as he loved (*Bible*, John 13:34). He added this one powerful standard to traditional Jewish law.

Muslims, too, have rules by which to live. "Muslim" means "one who submits to god." And Islam is the religion of Muslims. Islam means "submission." Muhammad was the Islamic prophet. Although Muhammad is not considered a deity (he is viewed as the last prophet), he spoke for the god of Abraham, his Allah. Islamic teaching provides five pillars. The five pillars are general principles or duties that are required of anyone defined as a Muslim. These duties are Shahadah (one's profession of faith), Salah (daily ritual prayer), Zakah (a required alms tax), Sawm (fasting during Ramadan, the holy month of Islam), and Hajj (an obligatory pilgrimage to Mecca). Subsequent to Muhammad's death, his followers also defined Sharia, or Islamic law. Sharia means "path to the water source." It is a set of rules that define acceptable behavior, and the rules are strictly followed by devout Muslims. Sharia was derived from the Koran and by Muhammad and his early companions. It has been open to interpretation, but for the most part, Sharia is a comprehensive set of standards for everyday Islamic life. So beyond following the five pillars which define someone as a Muslim,

Islamic law defines acceptable behavior for living one's life.

Buddha never claimed to be a divinity, but he is certainly a god-like figure. Buddha provided his followers with a method to achieve "nirvana," a state of being that transcends human suffering and provides eternal removal from the otherwise everlasting "samsara," the cycle of reincarnation, suffering, and pain. Buddha taught that suffering comes from attachment, and his method provides a means to detach oneself from all that one possesses, even the self. By detaching one's self, one becomes one with all that is, and thereby is eternally united to the universal. One way to understand nirvana is to believe that once achieved, a person is dissolved and fully dispersed forever in nature, which is eternal and painless.

Buddha's way to achieve nirvana is the "Eightfold Path." The eightfold path is a guide for those that wish to follow Buddha. It involves: the right view (see the world and others as they are, free of interpretation), right intention (be resolved and aspire to be the best that one can be), right speech (avoiding lying, divisive or abusive speech, or idle chatter), right action (abstaining from stealing, taking life, or illicit sex), right livelihood (working in an occupation that helps and does not harm others), right effort (do what is good and useful and prevents harm), right mindfulness (alertness, attentiveness, and awareness), right concentration (meditative absorption).

These guidelines are not viewed as absolute. They are not commandments, as with the god of Abraham (who is at the foundation of the Jewish, Christian, and Muslim faiths). Rather, they are recommendations from one who achieved a state of being that he modeled for others.

All of these religions provided followers with a code by which to live. They defined standards for acceptable living within a religious tradition. And a common factor is the identification of a community of "the faithful" that benefit by adherence to the code of conduct. People who follow the laws of their religions hold special status—as god's people, or as enlightened, or as moving up a caste hierarchy to a better place.

So why do people submit? Why do people seek god? Why do people act in ways defined as "good?" What motivates them? According to the ancient religions, doing what is "right" and "good" leads to special status, but not doing what is defined as "right" and "good" leads to a nightmare. There is hell. There is eternal damnation. There is eternal suffering. There is reincarnation into a worse situation, where one can become a pariah (born into the lowest caste—an "untouchable"). There is no clearer example than in the warnings of the Koran. "...and if ye believe and fear God, a great reward awaiteth you" (Sura III), but "Verily God will gather the hypocrites and the infidels all together in Hell" (Sura IV). And even Buddha, in the *Dhammapada*, warns of dire consequences for not following "the path." Specifically, in regard to violence against the "gentle and innocent" he stated:

Whoever harms with violence
those who are gentle and innocent,
to one of these ten states
that person quickly descends:

he would beget
severe suffering;
deprivation and fracturing
of the body; or grave illness, too;

mental imbalance;
trouble from the government;
cruel slander;
loss of relatives;

or destruction of property.

Or a raging fire burns his dwellings.
After the dissolution of his body
the unwise one falls into the lower world.

So even the Buddha, a peace lover and accepting guide, sets limits of acceptable behavior and threatens those who would do the unacceptable. These are just a few examples of alternative outcomes that result when failing to follow religious directives. A wise person does not want to take the chance. Since one can never know what is on the other side of life (it's a "leap of faith"), why not hedge one's bets. Religion plays a special role in this regard—it defines an attractive outcome in death if one follows religious rules.

So here is a basic rule of the ancient religions. Be good. And if you are good, even if you suffer greatly, you will find something better through religion or in death. If you are not good, you will suffer eternally.

The Human Spirit

I was always taken with the Christian concept of the "Holy Spirit." Of course, when I was a child, we called it the "Holy Ghost." The Holy Ghost was a ghost floating around entering people by way of their spiritual doors—their souls. I often imagined being filled with the Holy Ghost as akin to walking into a bakery and being filled with the sweet scent of freshly baked pastries. What a great feeling!

The Holy Ghost was capable of filling us with good thoughts and intentions and directing our behavior. He was a ghost that could enter us, take on our persona, and influence the course of human events. What a great god. Unlike the ghosts that the *Ghostbusters* (the 1984 movie) tried to eradicate (malicious devils), the Holy Ghost had good intentions and sought to spread a godlike message of joy, goodwill, and collaboration.

I was filled with the Holy Spirit at a Christian revival while in college (one of the few times I ventured away from the Roman Catholic Church). The music was engulfing, the revelers were singing and dancing in excitement, and I raised my arms in the air reaching out to the Holy Spirit inviting him to enter me and to make me whole. I was entranced, and at that moment I felt wonderful. Unfortunately, when the revival was over, I quickly returned to the same earthly problems I suffered before. Yet the trance was a powerful mechanism of escape. And I felt close to my god. What I really liked about the revival was that it was positive. I had so long been indoctrinated with fear—avoiding sin so as to save my tainted soul—that I forgot that religion could be associated with joyous celebration. At the revival, I got a glimpse of a positive psychology of religion.

Many people tend to choose to be good because there is threat of harm for those who are not good. It is a negative psychology, meaning people are motivated more by threat than by reward. A more positive psychology would build upon a system of rewards for valued behavior. B. F. Skinner, the famous behavioral psychologist, taught this through his model of operant (behavioral) conditioning. Positive reinforcement (reward) is powerful at shaping behavior. Punishment has negative consequences—a likely increase in aggression and confusion about the correct way to act.

In September of 1999 I attended (at the invitation of a good friend, Dr. Charles Schmitz, an expert on marital satisfaction), the first "Positive Psychology Summit." The Summit was sponsored by the Gallup organization. In Lincoln, Nebraska, psychologists from around the globe convened to initiate and to facilitate a movement in psychology away from focusing on the negative of human behavior (e.g., mental illness, depression, intellectual deficiency) toward focusing on the positive (e.g., creativity, intelligence, happiness). It was a very rewarding conference, and I embraced the idea of viewing what is valuable about human functioning as a standard. For too long psychology has looked at what correlates with or causes failure in human functioning. The theme of the conference was to focus on what correlates with or causes success (cf., Seligman & Csikszentmihalyi, 2000). If one is an optimist, one believes that people are doing the best that they can to survive within a given situation. One believes that, given an opportunity and a system of support, people will do what is right and good, and they will achieve in ways that improve the human condition.

I am tired of viewing humans as inherently evil. I am tired of viewing babies as stained by (original) sin. I am tired of dictates that condemn non-believers or that purport harm to others in the name of religion. I am tired of being threatened with suffering, pain, or castigation if I do not follow rules. Optimism has fallen on me as the Holy Spirit has fallen on Christians.

As a psychologist I have moved past the Freudian ideas that humans are inherently aggressive and sexual to the detriment of social relations. Freud's model is a conflict model. According to his model, each individual is in a battle against unknown, lurking, unconscious, and destructive forces, only to be overcome by reason. Reason is interpreted by a therapist, and of course the therapist is viewed as knowing the patient better than the patient knows him or herself. I have abandoned such thought. I now view problems as primarily social—problems in relationships. Problems are imbedded in relationships with husbands, wives, mothers, fathers, children, teachers, bosses, ministers, relatives, strangers, or friends. One can look at any personal problem and define its roots in biology (e.g., some people are genetically wired to be hyper, severely depressed, or sensitive) or, most likely, one can define the problem's roots in a harmful relationship. The times that I have felt most disturbed were those times when I was tangled in unhealthy relationships. Relationships are powerful at affecting one's mental health—for better or for worse.

Religion should foster healthy relationships. In today's

world, there is no room in religion for condemnation, negativity, prejudice, exclusion, or arrogance. These are the seeds of divisiveness, discrimination, pain, and hatred.

The ancient religions, at the surface level, do foster healthy relationships. A religious community is for many persons a very healthy and safe place to be. The problem is not for those who are accepted by a religion and who adhere strictly to religious dictates, but for those who are marginalized by religious doctrine or for those who have made a doctrinal mistake. Lesbians and gays raised in the Jewish, Christian, or Islamic traditions face this kind of dilemma. For example, the *Bible* purports that gays should be killed (Leviticus, 20:13) and someone who has sex out of marriage, no matter how remorseful, should suffer a similar fate. And the *Torah* finds male gay relationships abhorrent (Leviticus, 18). And if someone should be defined as an "infidel" in the *Koran*, well watch out! Diversity in ancient times was a threat. In those days, territories were not strictly defined. There were constant battles to establish cultural standards and governmental boundaries. There were strict prohibitions against deviance, as those who deviated from a social standard could detract from the work for the benefit of the tribe. But in the postmodern era, territories worldwide are fairly clearly defined. Today, there are fewer territorial skirmishes. Unfortunately, there are many philosophical skirmishes both within and across cultures. So one's religion and philosophy may play a major part in one's   acceptance within a group of affiliation or in a group one aspires to join.

The ancient traditions are based on doctrine that is exclusive and discriminatory, yet not all of the messages from the ancient religions can be viewed as unhealthy in today's world. Some of the messages from the past resonate. Some narratives from the past provide lessons that can be useful in a postmodern world: like the message of Krishna to Arjuna, or God's message to Moses, or the Five Pillars of Islam, or the Eightfold Path of

Buddhism, or Christ's eleventh commandment. These religions have some offerings that nicely fit within a more positive psychology of religion. They can offer more than freedom from pain, castigation, and/or suffering in another life. The adherents of these religions have survived the modern era, so their religions must have some directives that are valuable in a world that requires a high level of collaboration and cooperation. But the message should be consistent. One cannot speak of cooperation and collaboration out of one side of one's mouth while claiming special privilege out of the other side of one's mouth. Pope Benedict XVI, once Cardinal Joseph Ratzinger, Prefect of the Congregation of the Doctrine of the Faith of the Roman Catholic Church, wrote a document entitled *Dominus Iesus* (which translates to "The Lord Jesus"). The document was accepted by Pope John Paul II and became Roman Catholic doctrine on August 6, 2000. That document describes the status of the Roman Catholic Church and its role in salvation. The subtitle of the document is: "On the Unicity and Salvific Universality of Jesus Christ and the Church." The document is full of academic double talk, but in the end it clearly states that the way to heaven is through the Roman Catholic Church, the one and only Church of Jesus Christ. Each other religion is viewed as "an obstacle" to salvation, and other Christian churches have "defects." Essentially, Christians outside of the Roman Catholic Church are viewed as second class citizens. The document is inflammatory and arrogant of the Roman Catholic Church, a church that embraces the teachings of Jesus Christ, a teacher who communicated humility. The *Bible* (Luke, 18: 9-14) reads as follows:

He then addressed this parable to those who were convinced of their own righteousness, and despised everyone else. "Two people went up to the temple to pray; one was a Pharisee, and the other was a tax collector. The Pharisee took up his position and spoke this prayer to himself, 'O God, I thank you, that I am not like the rest of humanity—greedy, dishonest, adulterous—or even like this tax collector. I fast twice a week, and I give tithes on my whole income.' But the tax collector stood off at a distance and would not even raise his eyes to heaven but beat his breast and prayed, 'O God, be merciful to me a sinner!' I tell you, the latter went home justified, not the former; for everyone who exalts himself will be humbled, and the one who humbles himself will be exalted."

The *Dominus Iesus* renders the efforts of the Roman Catholic Church toward inter-religious dialogue (or even to Christian unity) less than fully credible. One cannot cooperate with others and condemn or belittle others at the same time without repercussions. And certainly, no Christian denomination should be uppity in relations with Christian brethren.

There must be an ideal that can guide without exclusion, prejudice, arrogance, or divisiveness. There must be a principle that defines a way. Postmodernism needs a "Holy Spirit," a spiritual guide in a world of understanding that comes from the power of relationships rather than concrete facts.

Welcome the "Human Spirit."

The human spirit is that which drives people to collaboration, cooperation, communication, and hope for the future. As a physically vulnerable species, we have survived by intelligence and by the ability to work together to achieve what is necessary to thrive. The human spirit is what brings people together against common enemies. It brings people together in love. It enriches lives through social responsibility. It advances the human condition through creativity, concerted effort, and cooperation. It overrides the aggressive and destructive instincts that served humans well in the prehistoric era. It is all that is good about being human today. It is embodied in healthy relationships. This is the spirit that guides.

I feel the human spirit when I join with others to assist individuals in need. I feel the human spirit when I celebrate accomplishments of people who have shown the way to peace, prosperity, and collaboration. I feel the human spirit when I make love with my wife, or when I hold my children close and feel their warm cheeks pressing against mine. It is with me when I hold my 85-year-old mother's hand. The spirit is with me when I offer my students all that I know. I embrace the human spirit. It is with me as it breathes through my relationships. The human spirit is with us, among us, and between us. It is not a ghost. It is real and expressed in relationships. I embrace the human spirit as I embrace others.

If we look diligently, we can find the traces of the human spirit in our shared history. This is where religions of the past have value in the postmodern era. They draw their adherents together in a common cause. Reflecting the human spirit, the ancient religions bring people together. The human spirit is the glue of human relationships. It is the deep and positive connection we feel with others.

Defining the Valuable

We know that we are capable of hate. We know that some cultures breed contempt. We also know that claims to "the truth" can be divisive to others who do not hold to that truth. We can destroy each other with the push of a button. We may be destroying the earth that supports us. We are embroiled in world conflicts involving differing cultures and religions. But it is not too late. We do not need better weapons ... we need better religion. We need to take the lesson of the human spirit seriously. We need a new moral and ethical compass that can positively guide culture into the next generations.

In a rich and varied world, having everyone reach agreement on all matters is not possible. There are too many differing situations, languages, environmental differences, and historical narratives to produce a singular standard of right and wrong. So we must proceed from the assumption that conflicts will arise. We must proceed from the idea that local truths (consensualities) will exist that do not easily interface. We must proceed from the assumption that there will not only be conflicts of truths (consensualities), but there may even be levels of truth that do not easily merge and that influence our daily behavior. For example, we have a socio-legal context (laws), we have religious contexts (church doctrines), we have prevailing community standards, and each may be similar or disjointed. People negotiate differing truths everyday in their relationships. The question becomes, are there rules that can guide us as we face differing truths at many levels? Can we define a set of principles that can help to ensure that, in the end, consensualities that help us to survive and to thrive as a species will prevail? Can we define principles that bring large numbers of people together in the postmodern era? Yes, we can. We can define general guidelines of behavior for the postmodern era and beyond.

We can seek a set of guidelines for optimal human interaction. We can draw from our knowledge base. We can seek guidelines from our past doctrines. We can build a set of principles that takes the benefits of the ancient and modern eras, and we can apply them to an advanced civilization.

What would those principles be? Although I recognize it is impossible to have universal agreement on a set of ideals, I am offering some possibilities in hopes that others will agree. A list of principles follows that I believe represents the postmodern ideal. To identify the principles, I set some simple criteria for inclusion of a standard in the list. First, the standard had to be consistent with the concept of the "human spirit" as it has been defined in this chapter. That means that there had to be a foundational positive attitude about the human condition and trust that humans can prevail through collaboration, cooperation, and intelligent, educated co-action. Second, it had to meet the criterion of the "Golden Rule" (more on the "Golden Rule" later). The Golden Rule states that we should treat others as we would wish to be treated. It is a gold standard of interaction, and it is found in some form in every major religion. And third, the standard had to be consistent with preserving or valuing life and facilitating human survival into perpetuity. To define the standards, I applied these simple criteria, and I searched the teachings of the major religions for concepts aligned with the criteria. And of course, my education (both formal and informal), my personal experience, and my professional experience (as a psychologist, counselor, and ethicist) speak through these standards. The standards were not divinely revealed. They are not carved in stone. They are relationships speaking through me—relationships with teachers, family, colleagues, loved ones, friends, students, ministers, clients, mentors, and all those with whom I have shared relationships. I hold no patent to these standards. In all, 12 ethical principles were identified which I believe reflect the ideals of religion in the postmodern era.

Loving relations.
Reverence for life.
Responsible parenthood and guardianship.
Respect for nature.
Optimism and faith that life persists through enduring
    relationships.
Valuing education and a scientific attitude.
Freedom of thought, speech, and communication.
Non-offensiveness.
Fairness, non-discrimination, and social justice.
Beneficence (do good).
Non-maleficence (avoid harming others).
Freedom of religious expression.

I believe these twelve principles can successfully guide humanity into the future. They personify the human spirit. The next chapters will explore some of these ideals in more detail and will make the case for a new set of religious rules for optimal human relations.

Chapter Conclusion

Given that consensualities can "go awry," meaning that people can come to believe harmful, hurtful, aggressive, oppressive, and hateful things within a group of affiliation, there is a need for consensually defined ethics to guide people. It is necessary to establish rules of interaction to ensure that people learn the importance of collaboration, cooperation, and intelligence for human survival and prosperity. Ethics are important because they help us to embrace "the human spirit," the drive to survive that supersedes the aggressive instincts (that served humanity well in the prehistoric through the early modern eras). The human spirit is embodied in loving relationships, in devotion to others, and in social responsibility. It is inherent and powerful, and it guides us to accomplish great things. It is the basis for continued survival of the species in a time when survival of the species is threatened by advanced weaponry that makes large scale war obsolete. The ancient religions offer much in this regard, as many of the standards of behavior that are part of ancient religious traditions reflect an understanding of the need to establish powerful connection within groups as a means to survival. There are rules to live by to facilitate human inter-action, and a set of such rules is offered as a starting point for defining consensual standards of behavior that can be taught to future generations.

Understanding "Bracketed Absolutes":
A Dialogue
A student of postmodern religion addresses her teacher:

Student: "I'm having difficulty with the concept of 'bracketed absolute truths.' How can there be limits to absolute truth?"

Teacher: "In postmodernism, everything is viewed within its relational context, even claims to truth. So a truth claim is always made by people situated within some social, cultural, and historical context."

Student: "Well, if that is true, how can it be absolute? Isn't it relative to its social context?"

Teacher: "From the outside looking at a group's truth claim, it does appear relative. But ... and this is important ... from within a group, the truth claim is viewed as absolute. An absolute is an unquestionable statement of fact; it is indisputable. So, outsiders view it as relative to the group. Insiders view it as an indisputable standard to live by. The fact that people will go to their deaths in defense of a truth claim makes it clear that within the group the truth claim is held as unquestionable. When people die for a cause it is reflective of action consistent with a socially defined and/or culturally held belief that holds special status to the believer."

Student: "So does that mean it is a universal truth?"

Teacher: "No. In postmodernism there are no universal truths unless everyone on earth would agree. There are bracketed absolutes, but no known universals. Even the truth of postmodernism is one among many competing truths with which people may or may not agree."

Student: "So being 'absolute' to believers in a community does not make it universal?"

Teacher: "That is correct from a postmodern perspective."

Student: "Thank you, Teacher. I understand and I can agree with your definitions."

※

Part II:

Ethical Principles for Religion
in the Postmodern Era

※

Chapter Four

Love and the "Golden Rule"

This Chapter:
- Provides a postmodern definition of love.
- Defines the importance of loving relationships.
- Describes the near universal principle embedded in the "Golden Rule."

There have been few times in my life that I have been touched by what I have observed in such a profound way as to change my life. One such moment occurred shortly after my son, Torre, was diagnosed at age 2 with Duchenne muscular dystrophy. Duchenne muscular dystrophy is a fatal disorder that is specific to boys and is passed from mothers to their sons (it's an X chromosome-linked recessive gene defect, and since fathers give their sons a Y chromosome, there's nothing to counteract the defective recessive gene on the mom's X chromosome). It is a muscle wasting disease, as the muscles lack a crucial protein (dystrophin) that preserves them once they are stressed. In time, Duchenne children lose all of their muscle use. They often do not live past the age of 20.

It was during my first visit with Torre to the Muscular Dystrophy Association clinic at Washington University in St. Louis that I observed a powerful expression of love. In the clinic I observed the love between a mother and her Duchenne boy, and the expression of love was like nothing I had witnessed outside of my own family.

The mother was in the hall with her son near a scale, and the doctor wanted a weight measurement on the boy. They had a choice. They could go all the way across the medical center to a scale that would weigh the boy in his wheelchair, or they could weigh the mother holding her son on a standard medical scale, and then they could subtract the mother's weight. Her son had an advanced case of the disease. He was slight, barely bones and skin, and she volunteered to hold him in her arms while she stood on the standard scale.

She reached into his wheelchair and was able to easily lift him into her arms. He was like a wet sheet in her arms, draped across her. She lifted him, held him tightly, stepped on the scale, waited for the measurement, and when finished, she lovingly placed him comfortably back in his wheelchair. I will never forget their exchange of looks during this brief moment. In fact, I was so touched with emotion during the weighing that I later wrote a poem which I hope will affect you as the experience touched me. I wrote the poem for my wife, Molly, on July 17, 2000, and it is entitled, "Madonna."

Madonna
She held him in her arms,
Thin, frail, weak,
But alive,
Like a sheet draped gently across her arms,
Her Duchenne child,
Dystrophic,
Transformed,
Transfigured,
As the body of Christ
Of Michelangelo's *Pieta*,
Yet different,
Because he smiled up to her,
Loved her,
And showed her life.

There was a powerful emotional bond between this mother and

her sick son. There was deep emotion expressed in that clinic, and I could not help but recall the feeling I experienced years before when I stood before Michelangelo's *Pieta* statue in Rome. The *Pieta* is striking for the depiction of the broad strong shoulders of the mother Mary contrasted to the slight childlike image of Christ. Some say that Michelangelo exaggerated his figures for effect, and in the case of the *Pieta*, the message is clear. It is a message of the strength of the maternal bond and the strength of a mother when faced with tragedy.

Jesus gave Christians an eleventh commandment—to love one another as he loved. In my view, nowhere is the love emotion more clearly depicted artistically than in the *Pieta*.

Being a father of a Duchenne child and a counselor who has treated children affected with fatal disorders has taught me an important lesson. Parental love is a powerful emotion. Nothing should stand between the love of a mother or father and a child. Nothing should stand in the way of full embodiment and expression of such love. It is a model for humanity.

Loving adult relationships are powerful too. Biologically, we are designed to fall in love. When two people meet and feel an attraction, there is often a powerful chemical released in the brain—phenylethylamine (PEA for short)—what some consider the lust chemical. A good dose of PEA in the presence of an attractive stranger can give one a high that mirrors an amphetamine high. It floods the sexual arousal parts of the brain. One feels good, strong, excited, and sensual. Relationships can feed off of the PEA high for as long as several years. Unfortunately, just like with many addictive drugs, a tolerance forms, and then one has a difficult time producing the substance in the presence of a past target of PEA's lust. Evolutionary psychologists, those that study behavior as it relates to survival of a species, believe there may be a benefit to subsidence of PEA after a while (usually around 2-5 years). It facilitates movement between loving relationships, because after the PEA high wears off with someone, one can more easily get high with a stranger than the former lover. And the more strangers one mates with, the greater the likelihood that offspring will have varied genetic make-ups. Varying one's gene pool is equivalent to insurance that one will genetically survive.

Some people appear to get hooked on the PEA high, moving from relationship to relationship, always lauding the most recent as "true" love, the final love frontier, only to fall prey to the inevitable hormonal lull that follows. Hollywood could take some lessons from the evolutionary psychologists, because certainly the love lives of some Hollywood stars are the equivalent of a psychology lesson on lust biochemistry. What Hollywood stars really need to know about is oxytocin, the cuddle chemical. It's the human bonding equivalent of *Superglue*.

Where PEA provides a hormonal high early in a mating relationship, oxytocin provides a nice feeling of belonging and comfort. This neurochemical is not only present in the loving early years of a relationship when the lust begins to subside, but it is present when parents embrace their children, especially when mothers breastfeed their children. It is the love longevity drug. It helps to preserve relationships for the longer term. But alas, the longer term in evolutionary psychology is only a few years—long enough to raise an offspring to physical independence. And then even oxytocin is hard to produce in relationships that have persisted well into the parental years. Time to move on? Some say the "seven year itch," popularized by a movie of the same title starring Marilyn Monroe, has some credence in the biology of mating relationships. After around 7 years, the love chemicals, PEA and oxytocin, tend to fall by the wayside in a relationship.

So what happens that helps preserve loving relationships past the neurochemical link? Well Charles and Elizabeth Schmitz (the authors of *Golden Anniversaries, The Seven Secrets of*

Successful Marriage, 2008) have been studying that question for some time. They have interviewed literally hundreds of happily married couples in long-term marriages to define the crucial elements of a long-term commitment. It appears that a long-term loving relationship transitions from a love fest to a deep, respectful, and attractive friendship. These people have learned to define their relationship as close and trustworthy, and they have committed to each other through trials and tribulations. They like each other, and they share their lives as best friends might. They like to be together, and they maintain close physical connection. These couples define their love as very rewarding. They are content, happy, and fulfilled. They have beaten the odds that come from their evolutionary ancestors. They are a credit to the human ability to establish and to maintain a meaningful loving relationship beyond the mating relationship.

But let's not ignore the obvious. Sex sure feels good. It's a wonderful natural high. If done in a way that avoids or prevents the preventable spread of disease, it is a beautiful form of expression. Sex is a basic need. We need to be touched, no matter how old we may be. Unfortunately, the ancient religions treat sex as if it is a horrible act. Some religious leaders remain celibate to prove their love and commitment to their god or cause. How sad. They are missing something very special. Sex is a beautiful form of human expression. Why make something so beautiful and pleasurable a problem? Let's celebrate sexuality, especially in the context of healthy adult loving relationships.

How is it that a healthy adult sexual relationship is defined as love? How are emotions defined? In 1962 Schacter and Singer carried out an experiment that led to their "two-factor theory of emotion." As part of the experiment, they injected college students with either adrenaline (which produces arousal) or a placebo (a no-effect injection). Then they placed students in one of two different situations—in a room with a person who displayed either anger or playfulness. Those that were aroused by the adrenaline defined the nature of their feeling afterward in accordance to the emotion displayed by the angry or playful other person. In other words, in situations where there is arousal, one defines the nature of one's own emotions based on the social context. If you are drinking alcohol in a bar with a bunch of sad people, you will define and experience sadness. If you are drinking at a party with happy playful friends, you will likely define your experience as happy. Two factors of emotion are arousal and a cognitive label of the arousal (you give it a name). That's the two-factor theory.

When we make love with someone and define it as "love" at the same time, it is love within the context of that interaction. The two factors are present—arousal and cognition (you name it). This theory of emotion fits nicely in the postmodern scheme. We experience together and we label our experiences, and then the label has meaning and reflects the reality we have defined within the constraints of the language we use. If we have sexual relations and during or afterward say, "It was just lust," or "It was a one-night-stand," or "It was just for fun," then that's different than saying, "We made love, and I love you." Love implies attachment.

Religion should encourage loving relationships. It should encourage healthy adult sexuality within loving relationships. It should encourage mutuality and sharing in meaningful relationships.

As to loving gay and lesbian relationships, followers of the god of Abraham find such behavior as abhorrent or worthy of death. It is no wonder that there has been discrimination against gays and lesbians, as the world's largest religions (Christianity and Islam) make it very clear that same sex relations are forbidden or banned, unless people are willing to pay a serious penalty. Hindu texts appear mixed on the matter and specifically address the issue of the "third sex" (referring to a number of non-male non-female possibilities). Buddhist writings do not clearly address homosexuality.

Although I am heterosexual, I refuse to view my gay and lesbian friends as defective or worthy of death or damnation. I care about them deeply, and I do not judge their actions sexually as wrong.

In ancient times there may have been some logic to condemning or prohibiting gay relations. Any religion, to survive, must have new members. Religions cannot survive with older generations alone. There must always be a "next" generation of adherents. In the old days if one was engaged in homosexual relations, one could not contribute to the propagation of adherents. One's seed or egg was literally wasted from the perspective of survival of the religion. In the postmodern era, such an argument has no credibility, as gays and lesbians can have children through artificial insemination and two gay people can raise a child in a religious tradition. Reproductive science makes ancient prohibitions of homosexuality and masturbation (another issue) archaic, yet contemporary religious leaders still hold these prohibitions as sacred. On the sexuality issue we have learned much.

What people do in private in a loving relationship I believe is their business, male to male, female to female, or male to female. I draw the line, however, with the spread of fully preventable disease in any sexual relationship (or in any circumstance for that matter), as I view that as hateful, and I would even go so far as to define the spread of preventable disease as evil. The AIDS epidemic is salient in this regard.

I hold no prejudice to love in any form, so long as people are careful and do not purposefully harm others. It is not love we should be against—it is hate we should oppose.

Love should not be avoided. We should be fostering loving relationships wherever we can find them. We should seek models of healthy, enduring loving relations and hold those as ideals.

Children also need to be loved, but not in a sexual way. They need permanent or long-term loving relationships where they are viewed with "unconditional positive regard" (to use a phrase coined by the famous psychologist Carl Rogers). They should be nurtured and protected and given loving care. They should be educated in a way that reveals and builds their strengths and encourages collaboration, cooperation, and socially responsible accomplishment. They should be held closely both physically and figuratively.

What we define as love can be considered a defining principle of humanity. Love may qualify as a near universal truth, as most people regard it positively.

The Golden Rule

The golden rule, "Do unto others as you would have others do unto you," is a theme that runs through the teachings of the ancient religions. It is in the Bible: "Do to others as you would have them do to you" (Luke 6:31). It is in Islamic doctrine: "None of you [truely] believes until he wishes for his brother what he wishes for himself" (Number 13 of Imam "An-Nawawi's Forty Hadiths"). It is in Hinduism: "This is the sum of duty: do not do to others what would cause pain if done to you" (Mahabharata 5:1517). It is in Buddhism: "Hurt not others in ways that you yourself would find hurtful" (Udana-Varga 5-18, cf. Dhammapada 129-130). It is in Judaism: "What is hateful to you, do not to your fellow man. This is the law: all the rest is commentary" (Talmud, Shabbath 31a). The golden rule is a standard in almost all ancient religions.

On the matter of the golden rule, we find almost universal agreement. In addition to love in partnerships, it prescribes a standard for all relationships. It is the gold standard of inter-action: a postmodern heavyweight. It assumes that one wants to be treated by others well. The philosopher Immanuel Kant called a similar idea, "the categorical imperative."

Imagine a world where people first sought to treat others in positive ways, or even to love them. If one enters relationships with a presumption that the other person may become one's good friend, then the way a person is approached will be engaging. Even in conflict situations, if one assumes the other person is doing the best that he or she can do from the perspective of the social and physical constraints imposed by the person's culture, then one can be assured that motives can be, at least from some perspective, viewed as honorable.

Views may clash. People may bring differing "truths" to the negotiating table. But a person's presence at the negotiating table itself is a good thing and may reflect honorable motives. If one is positive, one has hope that people can work through their differences.

The ideal of love acts as a "mind-set"—a starting place for entering all relationships. Remembering that first impressions are lasting impressions, a positive attitude from the beginning may be contagious.

What if we become frustrated in attempts to find loving healthy relationships? In the past, that was especially a problem. People lived in small communities and were limited in their ability to meet and to communicate with others. Rejection could be brutal, as a person could easily be ostracized by family or community. Relationships were often geographically and group limited. But in the postmodern era, there is almost 100% probability that someone can find someone else to love. There are over seven billion people on this planet; many people are connected worldwide with communication devices (computers, phones, etc.) that can transmit messages almost instantaneously. The chance of finding a "kindred soul" is very high.

If you cannot find someone to play ball in your backyard, go to the World Wide Web. My son, just last week in the Midwestern United States of America, entered into an Xbox Live game with kids in Japan. Incredible.

Today we do not have to accept rejection. We may simply

seek others in our culturally diverse and rich world with which to associate. In such a diverse world, we can assume that there will be social niches for us, just as we can assume that we will not fit well in other social contexts. The goal is to find a healthy person or group that meets one's needs for love and affiliation, and to sever relationships that fail to meet a standard of mutual benefit (applying the golden rule).

This idea has implications not only for interpersonal relationships, but for international relationships. It even applies across religions that seek reconciliation.

In the postmodern era, we do not need to have everyone like us, but we do need to nurture loving relationships and to identify a friendly corner of the postmodern world within which we fit.

Chapter Conclusion

Overall, this chapter presented an argument that love qualifies as a consensuality. Responsible parental love for children may be a model for all humanity. With adults, two people come together in mutual interaction in a way that they define as a loving connection. And, by treating all people as we wish to be treated, we establish a beginning point for all relationships—a rule of positive interpersonal engagement.

What Does a "Positive Psychology of Religion" Mean? A Dialogue
A student of postmodern religion addresses her teacher:

Student: "What does it mean to have a positive psychology of religion? Isn't all religion positive?"

Teacher: "Positive psychology is a movement in psychology that calls for psychologists to look at people as basically good and through an optimistic lens. It emerges from a history of psychology that is primarily negative or pessimistic of the human condition and of human nature. Positive psychology is an alternative to the pessimism of historical psychology."

Student: "How does this relate to religion?"

Teacher: "Well, many religions hold very negative conceptions of human nature. Judaism and Christianity ascribe to a notion that people are tainted by original sin—that at birth each human's soul is defective and in need of salvation. This comes from the idea of "transferability of sin," which means that our ultimate ancestors (Adam and Eve) made a mistake, and the human race pays for eternity for the error of Adam and Eve's original sin. Humans from birth are viewed as defective, so little babies are viewed as having tainted souls that must be rescued. That's a negative view of human nature. In Islam, Adam and Eve's mistake is held as an example for posterity; their fate shows what Allah does to those who disobey him. Allah is a punitive god. In Buddhism, one is prone to suffering and must be taught a method to overcome suffering (the Eightfold Path). In Hinduism, the soul starts at a place requiring hard work to maintain status or to move up the status ladder of the caste system. All of these ideas derive from a negative view of the human condition."

Student: "So you are saying that the ancient religions all paint a very negative picture of the human situation."

Teacher: "Yes. A positive psychology of religion would start in a different place. It would purport that humans are basically good (at birth and otherwise). It would ascribe to the idea that people do the best that they can to survive, and if their needs are met, humans are viewed as capable of outstanding achievement. A positive psychology of religion would hold to a concept of a human spirit—an inborn drive to excel and to collaborate and cooperate with others to attain mutual worthy goals. It would focus on the human capacity to love. It would be optimistic that the good that comes from being human will prevail and that humans will find a way to survive and to thrive, no matter what the challenges may be."

Student: "But how can humans be basically good if there is so much evil in this world? You have to admit, there are some heinous acts occurring at any one time."

Teacher: "This is sad but true. Unfortunately, many dreadful acts have occurred and are occurring in the name of religion. A positive psychology of religion would provide a model of healthy human interaction. It would not be punitive. It would not condemn non-believers or define them as enemies. A positive psychology of religion would draw adherents not because of threat of harm or condemnation, but it would draw adherents by a positive message of love, prosperity, an attractive set of principles to live by, and a promise of life in perpetuity through a network of enduring loving relationships. A positive psychology of religion gives each person something to live for and a code to live by without threat of hell, annihilation, condemnation, castigation, continued suffering, or rebirth into a worse situation."

Student: "But how do people become evil?"

Teacher: "They are raised in places where children and mothers are not valued. They are raised in hate and discrimination. They are punished unjustly. They are not taught a code that engages the human spirit. The human spirit is suppressed. Their needs are not met, so selfish acts provide temporary satisfaction at the expense of others. They have not learned patient collaborative effort. They are not rewarded for socially responsible behaviors. They learn hate and anger toward others. They view others as potential enemies and see human diversity as a threat. In other words, the seed of the human spirit needs to be carefully nurtured like a wise gardener tends to seeds in a garden. Leadership is necessary in this regard. A positive psychology of religion is the vehicle to move humanity in a different direction—it can provide leadership."

Student: "Thank you, Teacher."

Chapter Five

Reverence for Life

This Chapter:
- Gives examples of how ancient religions defined life in the womb.
- Provides a postmodern scientific definition of life.
- Makes arguments against abortion, the death penalty, suicide, active euthanasia, and killing through aggressive offensive action.

Some might consider defining the beginning of life a burdensome or impossible task. But the ancients did not seem to find it difficult at all. There is almost universal agreement among the ancient religions that life begins in the womb. The *Koran*, Sura III, reads: "He it is who formeth you in your mother's wombs. There is no God but He; the Mighty, the Wise!" The Hindu Shastras state: "As soon as the soul is released from hell, or from heaven, it arrives in the womb. Overpowered by that soul, the two-fold seed becomes solid ... it becomes a spec of life, and then a bubble, and then flesh." In the book *A Life of the Buddha*, it states that Buddha at the moment of his reincarnation "entered his earthly mother's womb." In the Buddhist *The Tibetan Book of the Dead*, the dying are aided at every turn in resisting entrance to the womb (reincarnation) as a means to make amends so that enlightenment may be achieved. And the *Bible* also makes it very clear—Jesus was made human by spiritual placement in the womb.

We can even look to the Hippocratic Oath, the pledge taken by physicians and thought to be written in the 4th century before the Common Era. That pledge held that physicians could not perform abortions.

Ancient ancestors held a belief that life began in the womb.

In the postmodern era, the question of when life begins has become politically volatile. No where is there a clearer clash of consensualities. Medical advances and technology now allow for removal of fetuses from the womb with few medical complications for the mother. We have drugs that will expulse a fertilized egg from the uterus. We can fertilize eggs outside the womb. And government and the courts have ruled that they do not wish to dictate when life begins, leaving decisions about abortion, for example, to individual conscience.

But in the postmodern era, we know there is no individual conscience. Individual conscience is a remnant of the modern era and the individual ideals of free will and isolated decision making. We understand now that decisions can be viewed as not occurring in one's head, but in the social standards and social relationships that surround a decision. Decisions are always socially compelled, socially derived, and made within the constraints of socially agreed-upon standards.

Two personal experiences have influenced me in this regard. First, I once contributed financially to an abortion. A dear friend became pregnant out of wedlock (it was not my child), and another friend convinced me to contribute toward the cost of a legal abortion. I did. Years later, the woman who had the abortion was diagnosed with breast cancer. She had no children, but was married. In a desperate attempt to have a child, she became pregnant while receiving treatments for her cancer. She delayed treatments that could hurt her child in utero, and in the end, the child was stillborn, and the woman died soon after. She was able to hold her stillborn child in her arms before she died. And the vision of that picture burns deeply in my eyes. I regret deeply my decision to contribute to the abortion, and if I had to do it again, I would do all possible to convince her to have the child.

The second personal experience was as a professional

counselor supervising a student counselor who was doing a training internship and had a client considering an abortion. The student brought an audio tape of a family counseling session to me to listen to and to critique. The woman considering the abortion was present, and her mother was present. It was a very emotional session, as the woman's mother (the grandmother of the child in utero) begged her adult daughter not to have the abortion, and to give the child to her. She pleaded with her daughter and promised to raise her child for her. She called the baby in the womb her grandchild. There were strained relations between the mother and the daughter prior to the pregnancy, and the daughter did not trust the mother. The daughter was also being advised by some friends who communicated that the baby would ruin her life and her college and career plans. The father of the child wanted nothing to do with the child. The mother made a powerful and emotional case to keep the baby, but the daughter decided, finally, to have the abortion. The student counselor on this case was pro-choice, but actually she did a very good job of not showing bias during the session. As a supervisor of the counselor in this situation, I took the politically correct stance, providing reflective feedback to the student, but I later suffered deeply over the case. I sometimes recall the pain and emotion expressed by the woman's mother as she pleaded and begged for her daughter to have her grandchild. I will have trouble remaining neutral on such cases in the future.

Abortion is an aggressive and a destructive act. I believe our ancient ancestors were right. I believe the ancient religions communicate a message that is crucial for survival of humanity. We must value life. We must value being human. We must hold reverent and precious our obligation to our children.

Interestingly, the ancient ancestors do not hint to a position about life when there is fertilization outside the womb. They make it clear, one has to have a mother to be human. What a powerful message. Mothers are very important. They carry and bring forth posterity. This is a highly valuable role. But a fertilized egg outside a womb does not have a claim for protection on religious grounds. An egg fertilized outside and existing outside the womb cannot come to fruition without a maternal environment. It is not alive unless it is in relationship with its mother. This is aligned with postmodern thought, where relationships are crucial to being human. The ancient lessons are clear, there must be a womb for human life, and this is a position that can meet the postmodern standard.

As a reader, you might think that that an anti-abortion stance is just a reflection of my upbringing as a Roman Catholic. But frankly, I am at odds with the position of the Roman Catholic Church. The Catholic Church's position is much more extreme than the position presented here. I am surprised by the Roman Catholic Church's position on life outside of the womb. The Catholic Church holds that life begins upon fertilization of the egg by the sperm, no matter where it occurs, even outside of the womb. This is a position that is not scriptural. I can find nothing in the *Bible* that would indicate that life begins outside the womb, but there are many scriptural references that communicate a message that there is life in the womb. Some have argued that the statement in Jeremiah (Chapter 1, 5), "Before I formed you in the womb I knew you, before you were born I dedicated you, a prophet to the nations I appointed you," is justification for the Church's position; but I actually interpret that to mean that there is a formation process in the womb for one to become human, which ironically can be used in a pro-abortion argument. The passage does not say, "Before I placed you in the womb, I knew you." It says, "Before I formed you in the womb..." A similar statement is made in Psalm 139, "You formed my inmost being; you knit me in my mother's womb. ... My very self you knew; my bones were not hidden from you, ..." This passage, too, implies nothing about life outside the womb, but it is clear that life exists in the womb. So the Catholic

Church has taken a position that is not supported by scripture that has serious political implications. The Church's position holds that life can begin outside the womb, meaning that human embryos or eggs fertilized outside of the womb are protected domain. This position is prohibitive of some medical research, like some stem cell research using embryonic stem cells. It is an extreme position. The Catholic Church also bans birth control (except natural planning), whereas, if one believes life begins in the womb, then active preventive measures to prevent conception in the womb are acceptable. In a time of serious and deadly sexually transmitted disease, the Church's position seems archaic. The Catholic Church's standards appear out-of-sync with scripture and the message that Jesus' life represents: he was made human by spiritual placement in the womb, and he was a healer.

The position that life begins in the womb does not lead to prohibition of birth control methods that prevent conception in the womb. It does not prevent use of embryos or fertilized eggs, fertilized outside of the womb, for scientific research to find cures to deadly and disabling diseases. It is a position that is justified on religious grounds (across major religions) about life in the womb. It is a defensible standard.

The position that life begins in the womb is a position that is not only defensible on religious grounds, but it is also defensible on the basis of a scientific theory of life. Maturana, who is a biological theorist whose ideas are at the foundation of a postmodern philosophy, also has developed a theory about life. He coined the term "autopoiesis" to represent living things. Autopoiesis translates roughly to "self production." According to his ideas, living things do not occur in isolation—they are in relationships. He defined three criteria for life (autopoiesis), which are simplified as follows. First, living systems are homeostatic systems, meaning that they find an equilibrium or balance and maintain an equilibrium even when faced by environmental stressors. For example, as living beings, we all maintain a body temperature around 98.6 degrees Fahrenheit. When we are cold, we shiver to warm ourselves; and when we are hot, we perspire to cool ourselves. We are homeostatic, just like a thermostat in a home which maintains the home's temperature at a comfortable setting. Second, living systems are not isolated; they exist in relationships to an environment. Anyone who eats a good lettuce salad with tomatoes and garbanzo beans can report being in direct relationship with the earthly environment. And third, autopoietic systems (living systems) make their own parts, literally. As living beings, we are continuously replacing our cell structure with new cells; for example, our skin cells replace themselves almost daily. And we are continuously reformed through replacement of parts. This makes us different, than say an automobile with a gas-combustion engine, which is homeostatic (it keeps its cool), is in relationship to its environment (as it guzzles gasoline), but it cannot make its own parts (wouldn't that be nice). Living things have properties that go beyond eating and breathing. They literally recreate themselves over the course of their lifetimes.

A fertilized egg in a womb meets all of the criteria for life. It is in a direct relationship to a maternal environment. It is homeostatic. And in relationship to its host, it certainly makes its own parts. A fertilized egg in a test-tube or Petri dish is not an autopoietic system—it is not in a relationship to a maternal support system.

Let's accept that life is present in the womb.

Beyond the Abortion Issue

A reverence for life position extends beyond the issue of life in the womb. It also relates to some other politically explosive issues: the death penalty, euthanasia (mercy killing), and killing in war. If one truly believes that human life has value, then one's position should be consistent. It can't be selective or discriminatory. It must be fair.

The death penalty is a good example. It certainly appears justifiable at face value ("an eye for an eye, a tooth for a tooth") but we have learned that justice is not always judicious, as paradoxical as that may seem. There are likely cases of people put to death for false conviction. We have recently seen many past convictions overturned because forensic science has advanced and is now giving answers to some questions that were not answerable at the time some people were convicted. Stories of past convicted felons being freed because new evidence shows innocence often make the news. It is likely that some innocent people have been put to death.

If you value life, you do not take the life of another. There is no prohibition in this for harsh punishment for criminal activity. There is nothing in a reverence for life position that prohibits offenders, especially those that perpetrate heinous crimes, from receiving serious penalty. But the line stops at taking another person's life. From a postmodern perspective, the harshest penalty would be complete social and informational isolation. Short of death, there are many ways to punish those who commit serious crimes.

Actually, the cost of the death penalty, because of years of legal entanglement, often exceeds the cost of lifetime imprisonment. Therefore, even political arguments in favor of the death penalty are vulnerable. But a life reverence position takes a firm stance that can guide civilized society. The message is clear. Life is valuable and not dispensable, even in cases of the lives of those who act criminally.

Euthanasia is another controversial topic, one that is associated with much emotion. Euthanasia is intentionally facilitating the death of someone (or failing to act to preserve the life of a person who desires to live). It is hastened death, and it is done with the intention of benefiting the person being euthanized. It is akin to "mercy killing." In some places, assisted suicide (a form of euthanasia) is legal. Assisted suicide is when another person helps someone commit suicide, and when a physician is involved, it is called "physician assisted suicide."

Euthanasia, any form, is inconsistent with a reverence for life philosophy. Life should be lived fully, and death should, when it is not traumatic, come naturally. This is not to say that we should not make people comfortable during the natural dying process. Of course we can honor wishes of individuals to avoid measures of artificial sustenance or heroic measures to preserve life. Letting nature take its course in death is fully acceptable when one values life. But to hasten death purposefully is not acceptable, if one holds that life is precious.

People should have advanced medical directions formally defined so that loved ones and medical professionals know their wishes. If a person becomes incapacitated and near death, it should not be a guessing game as to the treatment the dying person expects. Loved ones and good friends are obligated to get a clear and written message about one's directions in a medical crisis. We can offer each other nothing less.

Not only is assisted suicide prohibited, but suicide in any form is prohibited by a reverence for life stance. With the high numbers of teen suicides, this is a message we should want young people to hear. Life is valuable. If you are an optimist, you believe that no matter how hard life becomes there will be a better day. Even if a person's life is filled with pain, he or she gives others the opportunity to assist and to demonstrate beneficence, love, and social responsibility. There is purpose in life. We have a social responsibility to add to the cumulative effort to assist in the survival of all that is good in life. There is nothing more humanizing than aiding others in need. So those who suffer from disability, terminal illness, or serious physical or mental conditions all have a special role in offering others an opportunity to demonstrate their commitment to the value of life. Pope John Paul II, at the end of his life in his last public appearance, waved off those who attempted to move him out of the public view when he began to drool from facial weakness caused by his Parkinson's disease. He showed that he was not ashamed to be weak and debilitated in the presence of others. His message was Christ-like; it is a message that there is great strength in weakness. We all, if we are lucky and strong enough to live long lives, become weak and disabled. Negative attitudes toward those that are affected by disease or disability is reflected in a word used to describe them—"invalid"—a word that should be struck from the human language, because it implies that someone is not valid (in valid). Hitler embraced Nietzsche's philosophy that the "The weak and the failures shall perish ... And they shall be given every possible assistance" (in the *Antichrist*, 1888). We should believe the opposite of what Hitler believed.

Hitler, of course, brings us to the matter of war. Are any wars "just?" For much of my adult life, the United States has been at war. Although I served in the military (during the Vietnam War), I was fortunate to have remained Stateside as a reservist. I was a medic, and the closest I got to war was to see the medical ravages of war. The United States is a warring nation. President Eisenhower, who was a military commander in World War II, warned of the power of the military industrial complex in the United States. We have not heeded his warning.

At different times in my life I have held both hawkish views and pacifist attitudes. I have come to settle on what for me is a principled compromise in a postmodern vein. One should only fight as a last resort for one's lived territory. One should never have to leave what is one's necessary parcel of land to do battle. One should not aggress against others in offensive action. One should only respond in defensive ways.

I believe people can be ruthless in self-defense, in defense of loved ones, or in defense of one's lived territory (that land which is necessary for survival by way of basic needs). But I find conflict initiating aggressive actions of any sort unacceptable. People should be conscientious objectors to fighting wars in foreign lands. People should object to serving in military roles that support aggressive or offensive actions. People should resist the seduction of aggressive instincts and submit to the calling of the intellect in conflict resolution. If everyone honored the principle of non-offensiveness, there would be no war. In civilized society, conflicts are resolved by arbitration, not physical confrontation.

Wars represent the ultimate clash of consensualities. In the modern era, people understood their local truth as the only truth. In the postmodern era, one must entertain the idea that there are equally legitimate opposing ideas that have support within at least one other community. From the postmodern perspective, negotiation is a starting point in conflict. Negotiation should first focus on what opposing parties have in common. It's like two people in a foot race—what brings them to the starting line is not their differences, but what they share in common. It's what brings them to the finish line that represents the difference. Certainly, differences may be compelling. In the end, one doesn't have to surrender one's culturally agreed-upon principles in negotiation, but one must come to recognize the validity of the opposing viewpoint within its context. Ideally, unresolved conflicts will be settled by mutually agreed-upon arbitrators. Arbitration is when two parties agree to accept the decision of a third party in resolving a conflict. Arbitration is entered into with faith in the process and in fairness and reason, not on the basis of physical power. Unfortunately the physically strong or obstinate sometimes fail to show up at the negotiating table. Stalemate ensues (sometimes purposefully as a stalling method, as Hitler stalled and misled Chamberlain), or conflict ensues, or conflict is simply delayed until an opponent can or is ready to flex muscles. In effect, we play ape-hood games at a time when a mistake could mean annihilation of a nation, a culture, or even worse, the planet. In the postmodern era, there is no room for mistakes. It's not about losing some land or losing some pride. It's about losing a future.

Total annihilation looms over the human race as a reminder of the fault of the modern era. Our truth is better than your truth, and if you are willing to fight, our stick is bigger than your stick. But when the power of a little atom is more forceful than a big stick, it is cause for reflection. Nuclear face-off in the 1960's between the United States and the then United Soviet Socialist Republics during the Cuban missile crisis may have been a significant historical marker in the transition to a postmodern worldview. One is much more willing to negotiate when the damage of entering the war far exceeds the benefits of "winning" the war.

Negotiate first. Arbitrate. And only fight to protect one's self, one's loved ones, and one's lived territory as a last resort when faced with unprovoked aggression.

When is Taking the Life of Another Justified?

In the *Dhammapada*, thought to be the teachings of the Buddha, there is a passage on violence. It reads as follows:

All tremble before violence.
All fear death.
Having done the same yourself,
you should neither harm nor kill.

All tremble before violence.
Life is held dear by all.
Having done the same yourself,
you should neither harm nor kill.

Whoever, through violence, does harm
to living beings desiring ease,

hoping for such ease himself,
will not, when he dies, realize ease.

And the Buddha goes on to warn that doing harm to the "gentle and innocent" will lead to great suffering. And then he states that even a lay person, who is non-violent, has a special place among practitioners of the Buddhist method. He stated:

If, even though an adorned layman,
a person practices equanimity, is tranquil,
mild, restrained, living the lofty life,
he, having lain down violence
toward all sentient beings,
is a superior person, a seeker, a practitioner.

It is no wonder that we find less religious war-like conflicts involving Buddhists than just about any other religion. Following the Buddha's teaching, violence is to be set aside.

However, if one holds that life is valuable, then one's own life must be valuable too. There are those circumstances when people come face-to-face with death, and their own lives can be saved if they act to defend or to save themselves. In self-defense, can one be blamed if an aggressor is killed? If one's own life is in jeopardy, is it not acceptable to act in a way to preserve it, even if another life is jeopardized? This is a moral and ethical dilemma, and in such situations, reason should prevail.

It is reasonable to believe that one has the right to defend oneself, one's loved ones, and one's lived territory (that land or space necessary for survival by basic needs). If one holds this to be true, then there is no cowardice in running when facing a threat. There is no cowardice in relinquishing territory to aggressors if one has a place to go, to live, and to survive. In 1959, the Dalai Lama fled a palace and homeland when confronted with Chinese government aggression. The "fight or flight response" to threat is inbred in us. It is okay to flee. But when cornered, valuing our own lives and the lives of the people we love, we have the right to defend ourselves. We may be unrelenting in self-defense in those circumstances.

Certainly fighting in self-defense should be a last resort. It should occur only if attempts to negotiate have failed, and even then, only after every avenue to avoid a confrontation has been exhausted.

There are also those circumstances where choosing one's own life may jeopardize others in situations that are not confrontational. For example, a pregnant woman may be faced with a decision, when her own life is in jeopardy, to give up her unborn child's life to save her own. This is as complex and heart-wrenching a choice as could ever be made. There is little consolation in knowing that such decisions are never made alone— they are made within the language, traditions and interactions that come from one's cultural, religious, and personal contexts. They are made with the consultation of others in one's life. Such decisions are made in accordance with religious beliefs and standards. One is never alone in such decisions, and one should never be alone afterward. There is no easy answer to right or wrong in circumstances where one's own life is in jeopardy at the possible expense of another's. It is obvious, though, that one's religion is relevant in this regard.

Chapter Conclusion

This chapter has defined life as precious. It takes a firm stance that life begins in the womb or in a maternal environment that can bring a human to fruition. It argues against abortion, suicide, euthanasia, and killing (including offensive acts of war). It defends taking a life only when one's own life is threatened, or in the case of defense of oneself, one's loved ones, and one's lived territory.

Aren't Some Truths More True Than Others?
A Dialogue
A student of postmodern religion addresses her teacher:

Student: "Are some truths more true than others? All truths can't be equal."

Teacher: "Any value one places upon a belief does not come from some objective characteristic. Rather, a truth's veracity comes from its enduring application to human events in a way that facilitates survival of believers. There are, at any one time, many beliefs affecting each person's life and behavior. We live in a world of multilayered multiple truths. Some survive, and some go by the wayside."

Student: "You mean people are faced with many truths all the time?"

Teacher: "Yes. You enter into consensus with others many times a day on many matters. You agree to eat at a restaurant. You agree to be at a certain place to work or to go to school. You agree or disagree with others on matters of politics, religion, or personal values. You agree or disagree with politicians. You are in a world of consensualities and you engage or disengage with others as you communicate on such matters."

Student: "So it is a matter of individual choice?"

Teacher: "No. It is a matter of fit."

Student: "What do you mean by fit?"

Teacher: "You will engage or disengage from relationships based on the degree of consistency between your beliefs and others' beliefs and behaviors. Another way to look at it is that good fit is biological and social attraction, and bad fit is biological and social repulsion. With some people with some ideas, you will connect. With others, you will not easily connect."

Student: "So we go through life bouncing into others both physically and socially, and where we end up depends on how we fit, not what we have chosen?"

Teacher: "That's correct from a postmodern perspective. To the degree you consensualize with others is the degree to which you share one or more beliefs."

Student: "So we can be operating in multiple truths as we bounce around in life from one relationship, or set of relationships, to others, and we end up where our relationships take us."

Teacher: "That's about it. And the relationships operating consensually that facilitate survival carry weight. They will have enduring value until another truth begins to compete and draw adherents."

Student: "So even truths compete."

Teacher: "Truths do compete, and those that endure through lasting relationships appear to be the truest!"

Student: "Thank you, Teacher."

Chapter Six

Responsible Parenthood, Guardianship, and Social Justice

This Chapter:

- Emphasizes the importance of parental love and guardianship.
- Describes how ancient religions often belittled children and women.
- Demonstrates how postmodernism encourages healthy relationships, especially in child rearing.
- Argues that relationships are the foundation of postmodern religion and must be entered with respect.

I have had two extraordinary parents. I have been surrounded by love all of my life, and my parents carried on the traditions of their families by devoting themselves fully to my sister and me. My mother to this day has made her children and grand-children her highest priority. I know for a fact that my late father loved us more than he loved his own life. I will never forget a "moment of truth" in that regard when I was about 10 years old. My father, sister, and I went on a trip to run some errands on a winter afternoon. We had to drive some distance, and after one of our stops, there was an unexpected ice and snowstorm. The temperature fell precipitously, and the roads were quickly covered by thick ice and a very wet snow. We were on our way home. I was seated on the front passenger side of the car, and my sister, Debbie, was in the back seat. Approaching an icy snow-covered hill, my father got enough speed to get us to the top of the hill. To our surprise, just over the crest of the hill a car was stopped in the middle of the road. My father had to swerve to avoid hitting the car, and when he did, it set us on a course down a steep incline toward a one-way underpass with concrete bridge abutments. I'll never forget what he did in that moment of sheer terror. He pulled me to the center of the bench front seat, told my sister and me to brace ourselves, and then while struggling to keep the car on course, he said to me, "No matter what happens to me, get your sister out and away from the car and the road ... understand?" I said, "Yes." Well he did a magnificent job steering the car, first right, then left (by the book, turning into each skid and using the gears instead of the breaks) avoiding other vehicles, the curb, and street signs, and at the last moment we straightened just enough to pass through the abutments, like threading a needle. If we would have hit the bridge abutment, it would have been certain death for one of us, as the 1956 Plymouth we were driving was a death trap. There were no seat belts back then, and dashboards were made of metal. I know my father was prepared to throw himself between me and the dashboard at the last moment if necessary. I never thought of my father as a god, but at that moment he was my savior. His name, by the way: Salvatore.

As the father of five children, I have learned the depth and joy of parental love. I have known love beyond that which I could have imagined. Parenthood has helped to fulfill me. I cannot imagine my life without my children. I would give my life for my children.

I have promised to raise my three youngest children as Roman Catholics—a promise I gave to my devoutly Roman Catholic wife before we were married. I suspect she did not know what she was getting into with me, as she knew I was not of the Catholic persuasion, even though I was raised a Roman Catholic. But I have kept my promise, and I do not criticize the Catholic Church in front of my youngest children, although they know that I'm "not quite a Catholic." Someday, when they are older, they will be able to read my works and decide for themselves what they wish to believe. I hope for them that they come to value religion as I have. And I hope that they will find religious belief to be an important part of their lives and valuable in guiding them in an ethical lifestyle. In the case of my son with Duchenne muscular dystrophy, I agree fully with my wife that strong faith may give him solace and comfort as he (and we) will face great challenges. As a man who respects religion and as a person who lives among Christians, I know that Jesus will be there with us at our times of need. He will be with us, among us, and between us as we face or most challenging crises.

There is one big problem. As a father, I have a serious issue with the god of Abraham. I have problems with a god that associates disability with sin. I have a problem with a god that wants the sacrifice of sons as an offering of unquestioned faith. In the *Bible*, Genesis, Chapter 22, Abraham's god commands him to, "Take your son Isaac, your only one, whom you love, and go to the land of Moriah. There you shall offer him up as a holocaust on a height that I will point out to you." Abraham willingly saddled his donkey, and following his god's commands, he set up a place to sacrifice his son. "He tied up his son Isaac, and put him on top of the wood on the altar. Then he reached out and took the knife to slaughter his son" (*Bible*, Genesis 22:9-10). God stopped him just in time, praised Abraham, and blessed him abundantly, promising to make his descendants as countless as the stars in the sky. Little is said of poor Isaac, whose father was willing to kill him rather than even bargain for his life.

If a god called down to me and asked me to slaughter one of my children, I would tell the god that I would sacrifice myself before I would lay a hand on my child. I have no doubt that I would give my life to save my child's life. And I would be angry to be in the presence of a god who has no respect for children. How about the Book of Numbers (2:23-24), "From there Elisha went up to Bethel. While he was on the way, some small boys came out of the city and jeered at him. 'Go up, baldhead!' The prophet turned and saw them, and he cursed them in the name of the LORD. Then two she-bears came out of the woods and tore forty-two of the children to pieces." Or how about the *Bible's* Book of Job (1:7-22), where God gets into a little game with Satan, and shows Satan that Job is a righteous and faithful man by allowing Satan to destroy Job's 10 children to test Job. A famous line comes from that passage: "The Lord gave and the Lord has taken away." So children are killed as a sick test of faith in response to a challenge by Satan. And of course there was the ultimate betrayal of a son, as Jesus dying on the cross cried out, "My God, My God, why have you forsaken me?" (Mark 15:34).

This is all wrong. These stories portray an attitude about children that is abhorrent by any reasonable standard today. Any father that treated children like this would be put in prison for life. This is not the kind of father I want to honor. A god ought to be able to come up with a better way of proving a point than massacring children.

The Importance of Children and Responsible Child Rearing

We are educated and civilized people. We know the ravages of child abuse and a punitive approach to child rearing which runs rampant across many cultures. We cannot condone such behavior, even in the name of a god. Children are innocent and sensitive. We know that punishment without at least concurrent education on the manner of appropriate behavior does not work and has negative consequences. We understand that children are the future generations, our progeny, our hope to carry forward the human race. We must treat them with respect, loving care, and an attitude of positive regard. We must protect them from harm. We must prepare them both physically and socially to face challenges with intelligence and cooperation. We must educate them in a way that they are collaborative and non-violent, but they must be prepared to defend themselves when confronted by unprovoked aggression. We have lessons to teach them. We can build on a personal, family, and formal education to provide them with opportunities to excel and to thrive in a world that is continuously changing.

This does not mean that we cannot punish children when they misbehave. This does not mean that discipline is off limits. But it does mean that punishment must be judicious, measured, and always combined with a message and an example about what behavior is expected, wanted, and valued. It means that we must pay special attention when they are behaving appropriately, not just when they are misbehaving. We must reward valuable behavior. We must ignore harmless misbehavior, and we must punish harmful misbehavior justly, combining any punishment with teaching acceptable and expected behavior. We must teach children how to cooperate with others of varied persuasions, as well as to teach them how to collaborate and to work together to achieve attainable goals. We must demonstrate the rewards that come from hard work and sustained effort. We must set a positive example and communicate faith in the human spirit, so they have hope, even when seriously challenged. We must teach them the benefits and the rewards of social responsibility.

These are simple rules of child rearing. There is nothing complex here. Parents and guardians of children should apply these rules in order to prevent angry, violent, negative, aggressive, confused, and antisocial offspring, selfishly vying for power over others. So the ideal presented here—of socially responsible and educated parenthood and socially skilled and positive children—applies only to those cultures that value a future free of conflict, aggression, fear, and chaos. We want to avoid establishing a culture that breeds contempt and hatred as a way of life.

How many places on this earth are children neglected, abused, or treated as second-class citizens or as capital for those with less than honorable motives? Civilized people must stand against neglect and exploitation of children. Civilized people must raise the status of children. Children must be viewed as valuable and precious—worth more than gold or material possessions. Children are the future. We live through them. They are posterity.

Valuing Children and Valuing Mothers

To uphold or to raise the status of children, we must also uphold or raise the status of their mothers. Here again, the god of Abraham fails. Women are treated poorly in the *Bible*, the *Torah*, and the *Koran*. Women are viewed as vehicles primarily for the creation of male offspring. And only virgins have high value. In the "Extermination of the Midianites," the Bible (Numbers 31) states:

> The Lord said to Moses, "Avenge the Israelites on the Midianites, and then you shall be taken to your people." So Moses told the people, "Select men from your midst and arm them for war, to attack the Midianites and execute the Lord's vengeance on them. From each of the tribes of Israel you shall send a band of one thousand men to war." ...They waged war against the Midianites, as the Lord had commanded Moses, and killed every male among them. ...But the Israelites kept the women of the Midianites with their little ones as captives, and all their herds and flocks and wealth as spoil.

And then Moses, after becoming angry that the women were spared, commanded:

> Slay, therefore, every male child and every woman who has had intercourse with a man. But you may spare and keep for

yourselves all girls who had no intercourse with a man.

Women and children held a very low place in this god's eyes. And we find in the religions that derive from Abraham's people that women generally are held in very low regard. There are many examples of poor treatment of women and children in the ancient texts, some even too disturbing to describe (e.g., Genesis 19:8; Judges 11: 29-39; Judges 19: 24-30). Today, one finds egalitarian treatment of women only recently, and only among the most liberal of Christian denominations and Jewish synagogues.

When religious values conflict with ethical principles deriving from a refined understanding of human behavior, we must place those religious values in historical context and follow rather the consensual ethic that represents "a truth" in a postmodern context. We can understand how people of ancient times came to believe as they did. We can respect their local truth. But we do not have to follow an ancient truth that is abhorrent by a contemporary standard. We must reject, for instance, the inerrancy of the ancient documents. In a postmodern world, there is no concept of inerrancy. All judgment about error is made from a particular point-of-view within some socially defined context. The postmodern movement places all religions within their historical and cultural contexts. It does not allow for pronouncing universal truths. Understanding religion from the postmodern perspective allows for respect of all religious traditions to the degree they are recognized as local truths, not unquestionable facts. We can, therefore, limit acceptance of declarations in ancient texts that degrade or devalue children, their mothers, women in general, or others. We can subscribe to a policy of social justice, a policy that derives from Western culture and that is consistent with the postmodern emphasis on relational truth.

Social Justice Versus Oppression

American society is built on the principles of fairness and social justice. The pilgrims fled religious persecution in Europe. They wanted a new land and a new government that would treat them fairly and without prejudice. Early Americans established the principle of religious freedom, the ideal that all are created equal, and the inalienable rights to life, liberty, and the pursuit of happiness. They founded a country on principles of fairness and justice. This has provided a standard that all should be treated fairly and without discrimination. All people are viewed as valuable—men, women and children of all nationalities, races, colors, orientations, and creeds. American ideals are laudable and many have stood strong against oppression in order to establish a culture supportive of these ideals. One result has been that women in American society have attained a level of freedom unequaled in most cultures. From the perspective of children, that is a good thing, because half of our children are female, and almost all of our children are primarily raised by mothers. So we must hold women and mothers in high regard, and that will help to maintain or to raise the status of children.

Values of social justice and respect for others will not prevail if those values are not taught to children and embraced by future generations. Postmodernism is built on an assumption that relationships are at the foundation of all understanding. If we are unable to enter into consensus with others, then there will be continuous conflict.

Consensualizing involves at least two people defining something as true and then acting on that truth. It occurs when two people act in a coordinated fashion together around some concept they define as true. Behavior coordinated around a defined truth is an act of faith. No one person is more important, as relationships are between people. Two individuals are one relationship, and it is the relationship that is the focus of postmodernism, not the individuals in the relationship. Each person in a relationship becomes part of a process and all people in interaction contribute to the process. Each person, then, has value in the process.

If two or more people act to oppress one or more others, then consensualizing across groups around shared ideals ends, as one group's truth of oppression conflicts with the well-being of others. In other words, oppression occurs when two or more people agree that some others are inferior or not worthy of meaningful or fruitful interaction. Oppression is never one person against another, because the concept of oppression implies that a distinction has been made in language that identifies others as different in some way. If a distinction has been made, there has been communication and agreement between or among people that the distinction is meaningful. So oppression always implies that there is a group of people against one or more other persons.

Where there is oppression there is discrimination, prejudice, aggression, or exploitation. The concept of social justice opposes the concept of oppression. It offers an ideal of egalitarian inter-action, equal status, and mutual respect.

Distinctions can be made that either enhance or impede dialogue and understanding. For example, if two pairs of people are negotiating, and partners in one pair privately communicate that the other people are "a couple of idiots," then that distinction will lead to an oppressive attitude by the couple who agreed. They may act to take advantage of the "idiots." On the other hand, if the pair communicates that the other pair does not appear to comprehend for some reason, then they can attempt to engage in a different set of behaviors to facilitate cross-pair understanding and coordinated action. In the first case, a distinction led to oppression; in the latter case, a distinction led to re-initiation of negotiation by means of a different approach. The second approach has the potential to result in meaningful and fair agreement. The first approach will lead to an attempt at exploitation. Although this example is purposely simplistic to make a point, it is not meant to trivialize the very real oppression some people experience at the hands of their oppressors.

Social justice is an ethic. It is a standard for fair and humane interaction and negotiation through conflicts. In the absence of social justice, there will be oppression. Oppression always involves a distinction about human characteristics followed by an act of aggression, discrimination, or exploitation of individuals who are so characterized.

Social justice is a postmodern ideal. Because truth derives from the consensualizing process (the process of defining, acting upon, and negotiating truths) negotiation is best served when people respect each other. In the absence of mutual respect, the likelihood of disagreement and conflict increase.

It is the responsibility of parents and guardians to communicate the importance of respect for all other human beings. Children will come to value what is communicated to them through their language and culture, just as my language and culture speak through these written words. So parents and guardians have a special role in this regard. It is not the responsibility of the schools. These are religious values—values of the human spirit. They should be embraced in daily family life. We teach best when concepts are associated with interaction. We are models to our children. The postmodern ideal is a value worthy of expression. And at the same time we teach social justice, we show respect to the children themselves.

Ironically, corporal punishment has been an ancient tradition in certain Hindu ashrams (hermitages often run by a religious leader) and Indian schools and orphanages. This is ironic, because there is a concept in Hinduism entitled "ahimsa," non-violence. Yet, Indian tradition has held that physical punishment (abuse?) is the way to address misbehaving children. Apparently certain Hindu teachers in India have not embraced the teaching of their religion, and their behavior acts as a very poor model for the children they punish, which may affect the future generations negatively. If their actions are indiscriminant, non-judicious, or not associated with education of appropriate behavior, then they likely will have some confused, angry, and aggressive students. Hindu parents obviously must be willing to follow a non-violent path with their children, and they should feel free to address their concerns even to religious leaders who, for whatever reason, allow aggressive punitive attitudes and actions towards children.

We must carefully examine what we teach our children and what spiritual leaders teach them in the name of religion. I was appalled when I recently read a story in *Newsweek* magazine (February 2, 2009) concerning 20 Somali-American young men in Minneapolis, Minnesota who had apparently disappeared after involvement with an Islamic center in Minneapolis. One 17-year-old boy left his home to return to Somalia apparently to fight in a religious war. Another young man returned in a coffin, as he was a suicide bomber and killed himself and others in an attack. These are young men, children in many cases, raised in America; yet under the influence of someone with a religious message, they became jihadists.

These are extreme examples, but they demonstrate the power of relationships within the socially constructed reality of religious culture and religious education. So one must ask, "What are the values at the foundation of my religion?" If one cannot answer with the concept of social justice, fairness to women and children and people of every orientation or persuasion, then one must be willing to stand against oppression within one's religion or to affiliate with other religious people who will subscribe to a socially just position. That means, for instance, that women should be full partners in religious traditions and rituals—not standing behind some wall or barrier watching or submitting to men who have taken the leadership role and continue to make oppressive doctrine. If women are not involved at the highest level of religious decision making, it is likely due to oppression of women by the religion. Having three daughters, I want them to feel confident that if they want to take a leadership role in religion, they will not be second-class citizens.

Chapter Conclusion

Children are precious. Postmodernism is all about relationships and socially constructing our understanding of the world. All understanding comes through relationships, and our relationships to children are crucial to the survival of the species and to civilization. By valuing children we value the future. We have an obligation to protect our children from harm, and ironically, we have an obligation to ensure that religious doctrine or dictates do not impose values that are counter to the well-being of children. That means that mothers must be valued, females must be valued, and that the concept of social justice must be imbued in religious culture and family tradition.

Is there a Soul?
A Dialogue
A student of postmodern religion addresses her teacher:

Student: "Is there a soul?"

Teacher: "A soul is a concept one finds in almost all of the ancient religions in some form or another. As a Christian concept, for example, it is defined as a non-physical aspect of self. A soul is typically thought to be both a part of a self and transcendent of self. There is a similar concept in Hinduism called "atman," and since Buddhism emerged from Hindu thought, we find that Buddhists, except those holding to a strict agnostic Buddhism, embrace the concept that there is a spiritual aspect of self that is transformed (nirvana) or transmigrates (reincarnation) at death. Overall, soul can be defined as a spiritual aspect of self that in some way survives death of the individual. It appears to be a concept that is adopted by all of the ancient religions. For adherents of these traditions, a soul exists."

Student: "Is the soul a good thing?"

Teacher: "In Buddhism, if one achieves enlightenment, then the soul is transformed and becomes eternal and universal—one achieves nirvana. If one does not attain enlightenment, then one is reincarnated, and as in Hinduism, the soul (Atman) transmigrates, literally finding a new home. In these traditions, one gets another chance. In Christianity, Islam, and Judaism, you get one life to prove you are worthy (you follow religious dictates), and if you are good, you go to heaven (or paradise). If you are bad, then you will spend eternity in hell. Some people may live in purgatory (limbo) for a while, being punished for deeds that are not so bad as to require eternal damnation. One has to answer the question as to whether the soul is good or bad based on an understanding of how each religion addresses it. If having a soul leads to a good place, then one can say it is a good thing. If it leads to a worse situation, then one would have to wonder."

Student: "How can there be differences across religions? Isn't a soul a soul?"

Teacher: "Postmodernism teaches that there are no universal truths. Any conception of a soul-like aspect of self is unique to the religious culture and context within which people find themselves. It is, like all truth claims, a bracketed absolute— unquestionably true within a community of believers. So Christians embrace a soul, where Buddhists work hard to transcend something soul-like. Neither ideal is good nor bad from a larger relative point-of-view, but to see such concepts as relative, one must step outside the community of believers that hold these ideals as facts. Within a community, the truth is absolute as it resides within the brackets of social interaction of the group."

Student: "So postmodernism teaches that there can be a soul for some people, and for them, it is absolutely true."

Teacher: "That's correct. And their definition of soul will stand or evolve around consensual activity around the concept. For example, different Hindu communities may have slightly different conceptions of soul; so too for different Christian denominations."

Student: "So what I understand to be a soul really depends on how my group of fellow worshipers define a 'soul.'"

Teacher: "Yes, and you too are a part of that definition process as you interact with others in your religious community."

Student: "Thank you, Teacher."

Chapter Seven

Connection to Nature and that Which is Greater than One's Self

This Chapter:

- Explains that the beauty in nature resides in our relation-ships to what we define as the natural world.
- Defines nature as the host that sustains us—our earthly womb.
- Claims that we have a symbiotic relationship with the environment, and, therefore, we affect the host that sustains us.
- Argues against an external universal power in nature or otherwise.

I live in a concrete jungle. I cannot believe sometimes how difficult it is to find a little piece of ground free from the sounds and lights of machines. I have some friends who have a farm some distance from the city—they call it the "Heaven on Earth Farm." There is heaven there. There is no light at night except the light of the stars and moon. There are no sounds of roaring highways, whining tires, horns or gas combustion engines. There is the smell only of wood burning fires that punctuates the scent of the clear fresh airy breeze. One can taste the Western breeze there. It is a special place. At times it is bittersweet for me to be there, because it reminds me how far I have distanced myself from nature. I assure you, I'm no outdoors man—no hunter or camper. I'm a city boy through-and-through; but somehow I miss connection to the outdoors, especially when I am bound by my work to a sterile concrete world.

In my childhood in the suburbs of St. Louis, I spent much

time playing in the woods nearby my home. My friends and I had forts and campfires. We had hide-outs and trails. We had buried treasures. I lived a Tom Sawyer existence. My friends and I would ride our bicycles for miles to the Alton Lock and Dam to watch the barges and tugboats on the river. I loved being by the river. It was powerful, yet flowing. Finite, but ever-going. I was enthralled. It defined me. I have never felt a unity with nature as I have felt with the great rivers around St. Louis. Two great rivers coming together—uniting into something very special. The rivers were just as beautiful as they were scary. We knew their power. We knew never to challenge the power of the rivers.

And as the powerful rivers have flowed, I have aged. As I've grown older and begun to face my own disabilities and physical frailties, I wonder where I have gone wrong. Would I be in better physical condition if I would have more fully embraced nature in my early adulthood? I think of all the junk food I have eaten over the years—and then there is packaged food with preservatives, fake sweeteners, processed sugars, hormonally enhanced meats, fruits and vegetables, and radiated milk. I have eaten enough Twinkies in my day to be preserved in a plastic wrapper for eternity—so I guess I will have an afterlife. Who knows?

Seriously, what I do sense is that I want to protect my children. I want to help to ensure that the world they live in is not radioactive, polluted, sterile, electrified, or modified so that they are in harm's way. I have a sense of obligation in this regard.

To reconnect myself to nature I do a kind of meditative process that I call "centering." It has been therapeutic for me. It is a type of meditation similar to Eastern meditation. I use my professional psychology knowledge of hypnotic trance to facilitate a deep relaxation and trance-like state. At these moments I get a sense of connection to my perceived environment. I feel strong in my weakness in these moments, as I am totally vulnerable. But I can relax like at no other waking times. I feel hungry only for nature in these moments, as I am able to experience the world with full sensitivity—hearing, seeing, feeling, tasting, and smelling. For me, it is my way of reconnecting, as when in young adulthood I used to lie in the river on the river bank taking the river in and leaving myself there too.

I have come to recognize the value of full connection to what is perceived as natural surroundings. The native religious traditions play an important role in this regard: they guide us as we encounter the natural world. This is obvious, for example, in *The Cherokee Full Circle* (Garrett & Garrett, 2002), where "the creator planted a Sacred Tree for all the people on earth" (p. 63). The Sacred Tree symbolizes harmony and balance, and many Native Americans in the presence of the Sacred Tree "call to the four winds for the spirit of each direction ... to bring its sacred power" (p. 62). The Sacred Tree is considered both separate and a part of people, as all of nature is connected in the "Universal Circle of Life." The native traditions both honor the universal truth in nature and embrace its connection to human experience.

The native traditions compel us to value nature as a gift and to conserve the environment. When there are conflicts that arise related to human survival versus preserving the natural environment, I believe we have an obligation to make our best effort to correct any damage that is done. We can, like the naturalists, revel in nature and celebrate it as part of a new religious tradition.

Postmodernism is all about connection. Although postmodern knowledge derives from understanding in a social-linguistic context, we can also come to understand nature through the art, narrative, and rituals of the naturalists. We can honor nature in a postmodern context by establishing reasonable rules for environmental interaction. By doing so, we will likely enhance the human condition, which is intimately tied to environmental harmony.

We can accept nature as the host that sustains us. In a sense, the earth is our womb.

Isn't There "God" or "Spirit" in Nature?

To say that humans are of nature is to seem trite. I don't mean to claim nature by means of biological cliché. I mean to claim nature from the perspective of the human spirit. I know little of the native traditions or native religions, but I suspect I have much to learn in studies of those traditions. I do know that the native traditions treat nature as godlike—that there is spirit in nature—and that it is to be worshiped or praised. That is the message of the book *Black Elk Speaks* (Neihardt, 1932/2004). However, from the perspective of the human spirit, the beauty in nature is in the relationships between a person and that which he or she perceives. It would not exist "in" nature and "outside" of the person. It would locate in the interaction between each of us and the world as we experience it at any moment.

The interactive point-of-view is very hard for some people to grasp. They hold fast to the idea of an external power or spirit in nature or otherwise. Perhaps they do not want to accede to postmodern thinking, because it does require a shift in perspective. Some people argue that "god" or "spirit" is out there, and that postmodernism just explains how we experience it in different ways, depending on our culture and heritage. Those of a native tradition will experience it as a "spirit," whereas the typical Christian, for example, will experience it as "God." When confronted with this type of argument I realize that the arguing person does not understand—that he or she has missed (or has chosen to ignore or resist) the main point of the arguments of the relational worldview. I embrace these moments as teaching moments for clarifying my thesis.

The way I approach others struggling with these ideas is to have them focus on an object that is well understood—like a drinking glass. I ask them to look at the object, and then I ask, "Where is the drinking glass?" Typically they will point to the object and say, "It is right there." Then I explain that their answer reflects how a modernist would think. Following the theme of this book, I present an alternative view. I explain that the drinking glass is really on the viewer's retina — that the color and shapes that are perceived are as much reflections of the viewer's nervous system as they are properties outside of the nervous system. If the viewer wears vision correcting lenses, I ask him or her to remove the lenses and observe if the drinking glass changes. Typically the boundaries of the drinking glass become more blurry at some distance once a vision corrected person removes his or her lenses. Then I say, "Where are the boundaries of the drinking glass?" Finally I ask the skeptic if he or she could understand the nature of the drinking glass if I were not there to discuss the drinking glass. The typical answer is, "Yes." Then I explain that such an answer demonstrates that they do not understand the postmodern viewpoint, which says the drinking glass can only be known through interaction with another human being (in a past or present relationship). In other words, the drinking glass could easily be a hallucination, or it could be a flower vase instead of a drinking glass. So the drinking glass, from the postmodern viewpoint, does not exist outside of a person and it cannot be understood outside of human interaction.

So too, spirit in nature cannot be experienced outside of our nervous systems or understood outside of human interaction. Spirit in nature (or God Almighty) exists in our interactions and is not understood outside of the social contexts which define the experience. The spirit in nature is with believers; it is between them and among them. But it is not outside of them as an external universal power.

This is where the believers of the ancient religions or native traditions get stuck. They want desperately to believe there is a spirit or god outside of them that can be known. Passionately they argue for the existence of an external power that controls natural and human events. They embrace firmly the concept of an external universal truth because their training has crossed into the realm of indoctrination. When they make such a case, I ask them, "Why?" Why is it important to believe that an external power is in control?

Typically the answer to the question "Why must an external power be in control?" is something like, "Because it gives meaning to life." But I argue that there is great meaning in life from a postmodern perspective. The postmodern view gives us meaning as members of a community, as socially responsible citizens, as biological beings that have the capacity to love, to share ideals, and to collaborate to achieve lofty goals. The human spirit gives meaning to life, but it is not outside of us, it is among us. It is not an external power; rather it is in relationships. The relational worldview does not relegate us to a meaningless life. On the other hand, it gives us purpose in establishing loving networks within which we thrive and live in perpetuity.

Then I ask, "Isn't that enough?"

And if they say it isn't enough, then I explain that along with the great purpose in life that postmodern philosophy offers, it also allows people to join with others to believe in a higher power within the confines of their relationships, so long as they make no claim to a "universal" truth (a truth that they believe applies and should be imposed on all other humans).

Usually at this point their arguments fall silent, because they realize postmodernism does not negate belief in a higher power, it just locates it within its group of adherents. There is little for them to gain by purporting the universality of a truth, except prejudice. And postmodernism has an additional benefit; it provides a philosophy that defines the importance of relationships. Networks of relationships are greater than individuals, so they constitute contexts for expression of the human spirit and "a greater good."

Chapter Conclusion

This chapter makes the case for connection to nature through religious centering and full engagement of the senses in the perceived natural world. The intent of connection with the perceived environment is to find unity with nature and fully to immerse oneself in responsible stewardship of the environment. The native traditions define spirit in nature. But postmodernism does not locate the spirit of nature outside of communities of believers. Postmodernism allows for communal acceptance of a spirit in nature, but it cautions against any belief in a universal spirit or god-force. It also provides a framework for understanding that networks of relationships are greater than the members that compose the networks, thereby representing contexts for embracing a greater good.

Why Don't Animals Worship Our Gods?
A Dialogue
A student of postmodern religion addresses her teacher:

Student: "Why is it that animals do not worship gods?"

Teacher: "What do you mean by animals worshiping?"

Student: "Well, we do not see animals prostrating to a god. We do not see animals building monuments or acknowledging churches, temples, synagogues, or mosques. Animals go along apparently oblivious to religion."

Teacher: "Religion is in the realm of human consensualities. It is not located outside of language. Language allows abstraction and religion and gods are abstract concepts. Since animals, as far as we know, cannot communicate with us at an abstract level, they can never know our gods. Likewise, if humans suddenly were devoid of abstract language or incapable of symbolic interaction, our religions and gods would disappear and our activity would be akin to the activity we observe in the animal world."

Student: "So religion is in abstract language? Gods are in symbolic interaction?"

Teacher: "Try a little experiment. Try to communicate your conception of god to someone without use of spoken language or symbolism (no pictures, statutes, music, numbers, no mimicking prayer or prostration, etc.). Go to a friend, and explain that you are going to try to explain something to him non-verbally. Commit to doing so without the use of traditional religious symbolic communication. Following those rules, see if he can understand your conception of god."

Student: "I think it would be difficult."

Teacher: "Religion is in communication. Communication is in human relationships. So religion is in human relationships. If an animal could ever consensualize with human believers about god, then that animal would know god as distinguished by the human believers (or the humans would know god as distinguished by the animal believers)."

Student: "I understand, but isn't it a nice idea to think of a god that oversees both the human and animal worlds?"

Teacher: "You are describing a god that is an outside, external power. Such a concept is not consistent with postmodern thought. Everything in postmodernism is in relationships, so any distinction about a power would be among those who define power and in relationship to what they also define as an external world. Power, as a concept is redefined in postmodernism—it is not a linear force. It is distinguished only by interaction. Kicking a stone is as much about the stone as it is about the foot that kicks. Do you remember *Alice in Wonderland* trying to play croquet with a flamingo's head as the mallet? The flamingo did not cooperate. So postmodernism says power is not linear, it is in relationships. And postmodernism redefines "outside" as a distinction made inside of relationships. The concept of an external driving force is totally inconsistent with a postmodern world view. Postmodernism directs us to understand everything in its relational context. Even as you look at me, your vision is as much about your retinal activity as it is about me being 'out there.' No *thing* exists outside of relationship. The 'me' that you experience is unique to our human interaction."

Student: "So you deny an objective universal god-force?"

Teacher: "No, I do not deny an objective god-force, because in postmodernism objectivity is within the boundaries of social interaction. So people together can come to believe in a truth as if it were real. People can believe together that an objective god exists. However, postmodern thought does challenge the concept of a universal truth, unless, of course, everyone on earth agreed fully with that truth. Then truth would be derived from a reality rather than realities being defined through consensualities. What we experience, however, is a world of plural truths — many local truths each having validity within its community. There appear to be many competing truths at many levels."

Student: "I still like the thought of a benevolent power overseeing all living creatures."

Teacher: "There is much cruelty in both the human and animal worlds. The animal world is one of predator and prey. Death is all around us in nature, and not just in the jungle. Just look out your window and you will see birds eating live worms and bugs, cats preying on mice, owls and hawks waiting for an opportunity to strike on a rabbit or squirrel, spiders weaving traps, and other animals and insects preying on each other. It is hard to imagine that such a world was designed by a benevolent power."

Student: "So Darwin probably got it right with his concept of evolution, and using Spencer's term 'survival of the fittest.'"

Teacher: "It appears so if we are talking about survival of non-human living things. But in the human realm, the postmodern interpretation of 'survival of the fittest' does not apply to individual humans, but to a group of humans. Humans band together and survive by means of the group or tribe.

Human 'survival of the fittest' is about social fit within a group of intelligent, healthy, defensive, and adaptive humans. We call this human drive for survival in collaborative groups 'the human spirit.'"

Student: "Thank you, Teacher."

Chapter Eight

Freedom of Thought, Speech, and Religious Expression

This Chapter:
- Argues for academic freedom.
- Advocates for freedom of thought and expression in religious and non-religious contexts.
- Argues for freedom to practice religion without constraints.
- Supports freedom from religious oppression.

For 29 years I have been honored to be a professor. I have been in the enviable position of being paid to think for a living. I love teaching, and I feel a special bond to my students. I work in a place where the free flow of ideas is valuable. I work with others who are always trying to extend the limits of knowledge. These people are, in many cases, superstars. I am regularly amazed at the contributions of my colleagues to the collective fund of knowledge. I am proud to be associated with them.

It is not unusual to hear the lament of politicians over the lives of academics in public universities. Questions like, "Do they really work?" "If they only teach nine hours a week, what are they doing the remaining 31 of the 40-hour work week?" Quite frankly, I have known some professors who take advantage of the public trust. They essentially retire on the job, sometimes soon after attaining tenure. They sneak out to play golf rather than attending to their academic duties, which typically involve teaching, research, and community and institutional service. But these cases are few. It also tends to happen at universities that tenure for the wrong reasons. Intelligence, skill, productivity, and motivation should be the major criteria for tenure. The system does work in the majority of cases.

It may be that some public money is wasted on the promise of talent that is never fulfilled. But this is a small price to pay for protection of the truly gifted and motivated academics. If we together believe in the principle of freedom of thought, then we should support and never challenge their academic freedom. In American culture we spend billions of taxpayer dollars to build sports stadiums that are used sporadically for about six months of the year. Apparently willingly we pay athletes tens of millions of dollars for working a sport's "season." It is unfortunate that some legislators will, in this context, target some poorly paid professor taking advantage of the public trust as a problem. From my point of view, it is well worth the money to ensure that other academics are protected.

Politicians and religious leaders who target universities or intellectuals or attempt to limit the intellectual freedom of the brightest in a culture do so at great expense to their culture and to humanity. This is true whether the talent is inside or outside an academic or a religious community.

Freedom from Political and Religious Oppression

On May 10, 1933, German students and the Nazi Propaganda Minister Joseph Goebbels set books on fire in Berlin, proclaiming that the evil spirits of the past should be committed to flames. Prior to that time, German universities were some of the finest in the world. Under Hitler's rule, German intellectual capacity was quickly and seriously diminished. Jewish professors were removed from university posts. Some estimates are as high as ten percent of the teaching ranks were affected. Remaining professors feared their students would report them to Nazi authorities if they taught controversial lessons. The intellectual capital of Germany quickly receded, which may have been partly responsible for Germany's demise. When at war, one should want the brightest people on one's side, no matter what their religious affiliation. Hitler and his regime essentially shackled science and the freedom of thought and expression. Nazism was a belief system founded on oppression and the misdirected nationalistic pride of the German people.

There are times when religion can be as oppressive as political fascism. We see this historically in stories of those who offered opinions in conflict with religion (the Inquisition). We saw it in Afghanistan with the Taliban. Accordingly, the formation of religious states, or the mixing of religious and political responsibility, is a very bad practice.

On April 12, 2008, there was an "Appeal from Arab Intellectuals on Religion and Freedom of Expression in the Arab World" published by the Cairo Institute of Human Rights Studies. Seventy intellectuals and 23 human rights organizations signed the "Appeal." It reads as follows:

'The undersigned Arab intellectuals call on official and non-official religious institutions and movements in the Arab world to set aside the religious perspective when considering intellectual, academic, literary, and artistic expression, noting that religious guardianship over freedom of thought and literature harms both freedom and religion. It harms freedom because it quashes intellectual inquiry, curbs artistic creativity, and hinders the capacities of nations striving for progress. It harms religion because it casts religion as an oppressive, restrictive, authoritarian entity and gives others an ugly, backward, distasteful view of our Arab societies.

We urge these institutions, official and non-official, to focus on their original job (defending the Quran [Koran] and hadith from perversion), starting from the idea that clerics are advocates, not judges and their path is one of goodly exhortation, not burning, imprisonment, and murder.'

The Appeal clearly argues for freedom of thought in academic, intellectual, and artistic contexts, and it argues strongly against oppression in the name of religion.

It was in 1633 that Galileo Galilei was put on trial in the inquisition for promoting his views on the solar system. Apparently, in all this time the world has not advanced in this regard.

Isn't going to hell enough? Do people really need to be tortured or imprisoned for expressing opinions counter to religious doctrine?

The seeds of oppression in the name of doctrine were planted early in our history. The seeds have grown into weeds that have strangled humanity's march to tolerance, mutual respect, intellectual freedom, and collaboration. When one's view is held as "right" and other views are held as "wrong," one is more likely to strike at those in opposition. It is easy to control people with fear and punishment. It is quicker to control people with punishment than with reward. We know this from studies in psychology. We also know that the consequences are costly, as punishment produces aggression and fails to direct desirable behavior. It is more difficult to affect people through positive reward, guiding mentorship, and positive regard; but the side effect of a positive approach is a network of loving relationships, not oppression.

In the modern era, right and wrong were held by many people to be constant in a world that is inconstant. The postmodern alternative is that all views must be held as temporary—as means to possibilities, not as facts for all times. The world is not the center of the universe, at least as far as we know today. We must always entertain the idea that what we believe to be true today may hold little weight tomorrow.

Imagining possibilities, brainstorming, creating new ideas, dreaming, challenging—these are the methods of the postmodern era. Oppression, denunciation, threat, and indoctrination are the methods of those that hold to universal truths. So when I hear of mullahs taking over Iranian universities, I feel sorry for the Iranian people. When I hear of Pope Benedict the XVI (the former German Cardinal Joseph Ratzinger) discouraging academic freedom at American Catholic Universities related to ideas in conflict with Catholic doctrine, I feel sorry for Roman Catholics. Closed-mindedness breeds contempt for new ideas. Closed-mindedness binds one to the past and impedes progress, innovation, and adaptation.

Postmodernism speaks to the need for religion that accepts many truths. Postmodernism speaks to the need for religion that accepts each other religion as equally valid. But postmodernism also speaks to the need for values that support openness, freedom, unfettered communication, and enhanced human interaction—values of the human spirit.

People can handle opposing viewpoints. To truly understand a position, one must consider the alternative. If we really want to know freedom, we must deeply understand the concept of oppression. If we want to know the meaning of infinite, we must know the meaning of finite. Students, I have found, learn best when they are challenged by alternative views, even extreme positions at times. The method of contrasting positions is a means to facilitate learning, because it drives home difference. Difference is always between things and ideas, never within them (as Gregory Bateson so passionately argued). So understanding difference is important from a didactic point-of-view. It is a method that fits the postmodern relational mold, because difference is always in relationship. I have faith that people in general, and students in particular, have the capacity to collaborate in decision making when provided information that is contrasting, contradictory, or even non-complementary. For example, if one studies from the perspective of only one Hindu god, one misses the point of Hinduism.

Difference is valuable. Expression of differing opinions should be facilitated by religion. Jesus railed against the traditions and the hypocrisy of his religion, so, certainly, any religion in his name ought to have a mechanism of dissent. When dissent is squelched by religion, it locates all truth in the past and fails to meet the future needs of adherents living in an advancing era.

There is a place for those religions that hold fast to historical truths. Those places would be in isolated communities of believers that separate themselves from information in and of the new age. The place for such religions is not in the information age. A religion can't have it both ways—it can't hold to historical truth and also adapt to the information revolution at the same time. Because information is communicated best through the free flow of ideas, authoritative historically situated truth is not consistent with the free flow of competing viewpoints.

In America, we see attempts by some religious groups to isolate themselves from the information age. This is obvious in Amish communities and in some fundamentalist orders of the Church of Jesus Christ of Latter-day Saints. There are other examples. These groups have chosen to establish closed communities to practice their religion and their doctrine. They have a set and structured way of life. This has caused some concern, especially related to the Fundamentalist Church of Jesus Christ of Latter-day Saints, where plural marriage is practiced and there have been accusations of child sexual abuse within their closed compounds. These groups practice in a country where religion is protected, but they still cannot escape the law of local, regional, and national communities related to the safety of children, specifically, and American citizens, in general. It is a U.S. Constitutional right to have the freedom to associate (which also means people have the freedom to disassociate with religious groups); a person cannot be held by a group against his or her will, from a legal perspective. It is typically at the behest of people who have left, have escaped, or have been expelled from isolated religious communities that authorities have investigated the activities of those communities.

Generally, closed religious communities are attempting to avoid the information era and to freeze the community to historical doctrine. They are relatively static communities. For better or for worse, they have accomplished, to some degree, what many religions hope to accomplish—adherence to religious laws of the past in contradiction to advancement through expanding the human fund of knowledge. This is in contrast to religion that embraces the search for knowledge, which is a postmodern ideal.

Overall, religion must not impede the advance of knowledge, but the freedom to practice religion must also not be impeded.

Freedom of Religious Expression

Karl Marx, the philosopher credited as one of the founders of communist philosophy, stated that, "Religion is the opiate of the people." Ironically, as it turns out, his beloved communism has shown itself to be the opiate of the people. People work best when they work in collaborative groups (this is consistent with Marxism), but people work even better when faced by competition from other groups of collaborators. Marx missed this factor in his equation—competitive groups promoting competitive consensualities in defining what is real and worthy of resources.

Consider competitive team sports as an example. Teams of people working together can achieve great things, and the best of individuals comes forward when they work with teammates to achieve a goal. And teammates typically come from all walks of life, crossing socioeconomic boundaries. Team members know that another team is vying for the competitive edge. Talent is honed in team effort. Talent is produced when teams work in competition with other teams to some end. Marx must not have been a fan of team sports. He missed the obvious—competition does not produce class struggle. Competition is not one class suppressing or exploiting another class. It is not the bourgeoisie against the proletariat. Competition is people working together with people (within the same class or across classes) to define what is worthwhile, and then working in tandem, or in competition, with others who hold similar values. So when Nikita Khrushchev, former Soviet Premier, threatened in 1956 that communism would "bury" capitalism, he was speaking with a competitive edge while representing a philosophy where competition was squelched. Marxist philosophy purports that capitalism pits classes against each other in group struggle, whereas postmodernism recognizes the benefit for the group of intergroup competition of ideas.

Marxist philosophy has been at the foundation of political efforts to limit the influence of religion. Religion was suppressed in the former United Soviet Socialist Republics. The Chinese also attempted to remove the vestiges of religion in the name of Marxist philosophy. The Chinese, for example, essentially exiled the Dalai Lama from Tibet, as he fled from military aggression in 1959.

Part of the reason religion is viewed by some as antithetical to political philosophy is that religion provides a means of information flow unbound by state control. Religions have leaders, sometimes figureheads (the Pope, the Dalai Lama), and religious people may be guided by a figurehead, by religious texts, or by rules of religious communities to believe and to behave in certain ways. Sometimes this behavior can be counter to political dictates. Suppression of religion was carried out by the Nazis, the Stalinists, and the Chinese communists. In every case, political leaders were vying for power over the masses. And information and power are viewed as going hand-in-hand. But the postmodern view of power is different than what we have experienced in the modern era.

Power is a unidirectional concept. Power implies unilateral force or influence. It results from action and, at face value, it produces reaction. The focus in any analysis of power is usually the actor—as the actor is viewed as an instigator or director. Power is a linear concept.

In the postmodern era, the concept of power is redefined in the context of relationships. You may think you have power when you kick a frog and it hops away. But what happens when you kick a rattlesnake? You may think you have power when you threaten an Amish family and they submit. But what happens when you threaten a Mafia family? Who has the power in this situation? According to postmodern thought, unilateral power is an illusion. Certainly one can threaten an unarmed person with death or pain, but the consequence of the threat may be different than what is locally observed as an outcome. The Dalai Lama fled the Chinese army, but the Dalai Lama's influence on human affairs, or even Chinese policy, may be enhanced in his exile. His influence may be greater than it could have ever been if he was isolated in a palace in Tibet.

Differentially, to analyze power one must take a relational view. There are stories throughout history of the illusion of power, such as David and Goliath and the war between the Spartans and the Athenians. In those cases, the predicted victor took a hard fall. Certainly one should not jump to conclusions. In a relational world, activity in one part of the web reverberates in other parts of the web, and the effect tends to be recursive rather than linear. Who would have guessed that a Roman governor at the height of the Roman Empire would kill a young Jewish rabbi only to have the rabbi have a greater influence over the course of history than the Roman Empire?

Because acting on belief is what makes us human, suppression of belief is the equivalent of trying to dam a raging river with a few twigs. Suppression of belief is suppression of the human spirit—that collaborative, cooperative, competitive drive that supersedes even the most basic human instincts. Suppression of belief forces our most human process under-ground. It is not enough to substitute politics for religious philosophy, because politics is the science of resource allocation, and painful decisions about benefits for some at costs to others will be made. Religion offers an escape from suffering and pain. It is equivalent to getting a massage after a hard day's work. It entrances, refreshes, and re-invigorates. Politics is too sobering to take the place of religion. It is adversarial, especially in times of limited resources. Within one's religion, there should be a place free of adversity and full of hope. Marx saw religion as numbing. It is just the opposite: religion is revitalizing. Religion acts as a complement to politics, so long as politicians and religious leaders maintain a healthy degree of respect for each other and so long as there is a formal political and resource separation of church and state.

Chapter Conclusion

This chapter has argued that religion should not be oppressive and should not take on a political role. The idea of the founders of the United States of America that "church and state" should be separate was a very good idea. This chapter has also presented the case that each person should be free to express him or herself through religion. There have been times when political philosophy has favored limits on religious freedom (as in the former Soviet Republics). The negative consequences of both limits on religious freedom and oppressive religious political doctrine were explored.

Understanding "Spiritual Seeking":
A Dialogue
A student of postmodern religion addresses her teacher:

Student: "What is a 'spiritual seeker?'"

Teacher: "I have heard the term, and my understanding is that some people agree with a philosophy of life that values self and religious exploration as a means to an end. They seek to explore many religious doctrines and personal philosophies, holding the process of seeking as worthwhile. That's my understanding."

Student: "From a postmodern perspective, is there value in such a search?"

Teacher: "Value derives from agreement by those who propose, disseminate, subscribe to, or practice a philosophy or doctrine. Spiritual seeking is held by spiritual seekers as valuable, or they wouldn't act in accordance with such an idea. It is no more valuable than any belief system, and it certainly, at face value, does not appear to be a harmful way to believe."

Student: "But isn't there danger in that they never know a truth?"

Teacher: "Seekers know the truth of the search—that's what they define as 'a truth.' To them, spirituality is a journey, not an end. They celebrate a life of exploration, not religious demarcation. Some spiritual seekers probably find an acceptable religious truth other than seeking, in which case they would culminate their journeys and subscribe to a set belief system other than seeking. Some spiritual seekers may affiliate with religious traditions in the end. Others may go to their deaths as journeyers and explorers of truth."

Student: "Will they be satisfied?"

Teacher: "Only they can answer that question."

Student: "Thank you, Teacher."

Chapter Nine

Doing Good, Avoiding Evil, and Making Decisions

This Chapter:
- Defines the ethical principles of beneficence (doing good) and non-maleficence (avoiding evil).
- Describes decision making as a social process—not a process in one's head.

Most people agree that there is evil in this world. One can turn on the television news, read the newspaper, or check a computer linked to the World Wide Web and hear or see horror stories of people doing harm to each other, abuse of children, dreadful diseases, and reports of restricted freedom at the hands of those that wield power unjustly. Any socially just code of conduct, any standard that holds human life and freedom of thought as valuable, must ascribe to directives that require that people first act to do no harm and, additionally, to benefit others as they benefit themselves. Historically, the directives to do no harm and to benefit others have been characterized in two related terms: non-maleficence and beneficence.

Non-maleficence (doing no harm) and beneficence (doing good for others) are two of the oldest standards of ethical practice on earth. For example, they are referenced in the Hippocratic Oath, the oath taken by physicians upon their admission to their profession. The Hippocratic Oath is thought to have been written in the 4th century before the Common Era. For as long as we have known, physicians have been held to a high standard of behavior.

As with most concepts in human language, beneficence and

non-maleficence are both contrasting and complementary. We understand one better by comprehending the other.

Beneficence is the more positive concept. It reflects the positive attitude of the human spirit. Be good in relation to others. Act in the best interest of others. Take the well-being of others to heart. Assist others in need. These are the directives of the ethical principle of beneficence. It is a principle that is embraced by the helping professions, such as medicine, nursing, psychology, counseling, social work, and others. It is a principle that everyone should embrace as a standard of human inter-action. At the very moment I was writing this paragraph sitting in a local restaurant, an elderly woman fell to the floor while getting up from her table. Several strangers got up from their tables and went to her aid. She was unharmed but a little emotionally shaken, and others stayed with her until she indicated she was alright. This is the human spirit at work. This is beneficence.

The human spirit teaches that beneficence does not come at self-expense. In other words, when we act for the well-being of others it does not mean that we are acting in a way that is detri-mental to self. We can benefit ourselves by helping others. Physicians, for example, are highly paid professionals who make a good living assisting others in need. Most professions can be viewed the same way. People who construct homes or cars for a living benefit themselves when they build a quality and safe product for others. So long as professionals do not act to exploit the consumer, the actions of professionals all add to a larger benefit to other individuals and society. Providing a useful product or service is valuable and beneficial. A wise business person builds a reputation of fair practice and honest dealing with customers. The short-term benefits of cheating may well be overridden by the long-term detriments that derive from cheating; early in a career exploitation of others will likely prove counter-productive. By doing work well and dealing fairly with others, our services and products become valuable and they add to the collective well-being of all involved parties. And of course, we should not be involved in work that does detriment to others—that purposefully exploits others for one's own benefit. Selling substances of abuse, taking advantage of workers by not paying a decent wage, exploitation of children, and pollution of the environment are examples of actions by those who seek quick returns at the expense of others. The concept of beneficence, as you can see, is closely associated with the need to be non-maleficent—to do no harm.

Beneficence is an active concept. We are directed to do something—to act. We are compelled by beneficence to actively seek to help others. Non-maleficence, by means of contrast, is a passive concept—we are compelled to avoid harming others. When the little devil appears on one's shoulder (aside the little angel on the other shoulder) one is obligated to ignore the directive to do harm. Non-maleficence is a concept that directs us to avoid evil. It directs inactivity when there is an option to do something selfish and socially irresponsible. We must not listen to the devils on our shoulders. We must not allow selfish instincts to supersede the benefits for others and ourselves that come from socially responsible behavior.

Choices arise. People are often at crossroads. Quandaries present themselves. What should one do? The concepts of beneficence and non-maleficence are helpful in this regard.

In social psychology, there have been a number of experiments under the heading of "primrose path" experiments or "prisoner's dilemma" experiments that test whether people will choose a selfish behavior or an altruistic (mutual benefit) behavior when forced to choose. The selfish choice typically has some benefits—more money for example. The altruistic choice typically pays less, but if everyone accedes to the altruistic choice, the players actually have the greatest chance of gain. Sometimes people don't see that by collaborating, in the end they have the most to gain. Winners do take all in some situations, but in many situations, more have the most to gain by working together to some mutual end. Social responsibility has its rewards.

Addressing Evil

Some of us face evil more than others. Some of us are faced daily with challenges of those who would abuse or exploit us. Some face circumstances that do not allow for escaping conditions that are harmful or even deadly. Some face circumstances that do not allow for remedies or prevention of even common illnesses or disease. A good portion of humanity is suffering and in pain. Selfishness is, at face value, the answer—looking out for number one—seeking satisfaction of one's own needs no matter what the cost to others. But selfishness only goes so far. It is a quick fix, typically without long-term benefits.

How can one escape poverty, oppression, or environments that breed contempt, selfishness and ignorance? How can one escape deadly environments to find a better place—to be accepted and nurtured in loving relations? How can one escape plagues and epidemics to provide safety for one's loved ones? We can agree there is evil in this world, and people of reason must stand for and promulgate a new standard of behavior that is modeled in the human spirit. Those that hold to the directive of the human spirit can provide a new ethic—a new moral ground—upon which all people can stand together to address the evils in this world. By expanding the network of loving relations, evil will be circumscribed. In the end, with patience, the human spirit will prevail.

If there is to be contagion, let it be the contagion of the human spirit. We have something to say in this. We, if guided by beneficence, can act to spread the good news that comes from the postmodern ethic. We can make a difference by joining with others to act by a new set of standards and by spreading the positive message of the human spirit. The golden rule guides us. Collaboration and cooperation can supersede even the most basic selfish instincts. Alternatives to evil are compelling, and it is imperative that the message is disseminated. This should be the message of religion in the postmodern era.

Is Deciding to Do Good an Individual Choice?

Sometimes I fall prey to my indoctrination in modernist thought. For example, my socialization in modernist thought came through the metaphor used earlier in this chapter. That metaphor was the story of a little devil on one shoulder arguing against the little angel on one's other shoulder to get the decision-making "head" to take sides.

I've seen this cartoonesque image on television, in movies, and in pictures. It is part of the American cultural landscape. It is an excellent example of how Freudian theory pervades our everyday understanding of behavior. The little devil represents our most basic drives for sex and aggression—it is the "id" of Freudian theory (that part of the psyche linked to our most basic needs to survive and to reproduce). Then there is the little angel on the other shoulder, representing our moral conscience—it is the superego of Freudian theory (that part of our psyche linked to social responsibility). Of course the head in the middle represents the rational mediator—that is the ego in Freudian theory (the part of the psyche that moderates the conflict between basic drives and one's moral conscience). The idea that there is an individual head making a decision is classic psychological thinking. It is reification of "the individual" through the invisible, yet influential "psyche." That is about as modernist as one can get in one's understanding of decision making.

When I have been confronted most vehemently by others about the faults of postmodernism, it is on the matter of individual choice and one's individual freedom to make decisions. There is no individual choice in postmodern philosophy. Choice is always a representation of one's social, societal, and cultural history and the influence of past and current relationships. Often there is some biology involved too. So when you "decide" to drive into McDonald's for a Big Mac, fries, and a sweet soda instead of stopping at the fruit stand for lunch, that is your culture in full engagement. You have been flooded with images of golden arches, the sounds of catchy tunes, and pictures of juicy hamburgers. The voices of your choice are the voices of the people who own McDonald's, who manage the company, who produced the food, who marketed the products, and who serve it up with a smile. As one of my psychology professors once taught, "If you want to have a successful restaurant, serve sugar, salt, and fat" (three natural reinforcers). There's no shortage of sugar, salt, and fat at McDonald's. So you think you made a freely determined decision to eat lunch at McDonald's, but there was no decision made in your head. Going to McDonald's was a "no-brainer." It's one's American culture speaking through one's actions. It is an example of a highly culturally influenced behavior that looks to modernist thinkers like some sort of individual choice.

All decisions are socially and biologically compelled and socially derived. As examples, one does not choose a spouse, a school, or a career outside of interaction. Biology may compel a decision, such as with whom one mates, but in the end, there is interaction which influences the outcome. When choosing a spouse, for example, biology may be a powerful factor early in the relationship, but other factors come into play; the influence of both partners' families, friends, and cultures all speak aside the biological in establishing a consensual relationship. That's why some encourage young couples to get to know each other well before deciding to marry—not to rush into marriage—thereby allowing social factors to evolve.

Some may argue that their decisions were made by free will. But free will is a culturally loaded Western concept. (In Eastern cultures, decision making has been viewed as more "collectivist," meaning that a collection of people composing a social group has influence over the decision). A choice made by what some people call "free will" is simply a choice made counter to the advice of some others, but consistent with a consensus none-the-less.

I often ask my students how it happened that they chose to attend their undergraduate college. Inevitably their choice was influenced by a high school counselor who presented materials on the college, a family member or friend who told them about the school, or some impressive communication about a program, philosophy, or religion associated with the school. Choice of a college is never made in isolation or without communication.

The choices that brought you where you are today were likely influenced powerfully by your relationships. So choosing good and avoiding evil is not about a decision made in one's head. It reflects the operation of one's social matrix.

The messages of beneficence and non-maleficence have been presented to you. You are interacting now, by reading these pages, with someone who is engaged in a network established to follow beneficent and non-maleficent ethical imperatives. There are other networks that will align with you if you too communicate these ideals. The greater your connection to a loving, benevolent, and caring community, the more it will look like choosing good and avoiding evil were easy decisions.

Communicating with others on matters of social responsibility and principles of the human spirit will result in immersion in a group of those that hold similar ideals. Immersion through communication within a caring community is the postmodern equivalent of choosing good over evil. To associate with "good," one must simply communicate the message, and others of the same persuasion will be attracted (like a magnet attracts). Likewise, one should challenge the message of those who speak a maleficent point-of-view, and avoidance of them will happen like a magnet repulses. It's not about choice (as in the psychology of the individual); it is about engaging in relationships with those living an ethical lifestyle and the process of disengaging from relationships that would lead one down an evil path.

Astute parents generally know that decisions are biologically and socially compelled and influenced. They often must confront the influence of a child's peer group that may not mesh well with the family's cultural traditions, especially when children reach the teenage years and their needs can no longer be met within the family. Astute parents work hard to connect their children to groups of influence consistent with family ideals—with school sports teams, musical groups (bands or choirs), church groups, and social groups that link their child to the traditions that have positive connections to a support community. A parent's nightmare is having a child disengage from healthy family and community relationships to engage with others who will connect the child to groups that do not interact or interface well with family members or family systems. These groups may be counter to the influence of the family, or to the extreme, they may be socially repulsive to members of the family of origin. Consider the drug culture as an example. Educated parents in a drug prohibitionist culture work hard to connect their children to groups that also prohibit or discourage drug use. A child's connection to a relationship of influence where drugs are viewed as fun and safe can potentially connect the child to a group of influence that does not interface with the family culture. Conflicting consensualities (competing bracketed absolute truths) ensue when one group is connected to a group holding conflicting ideals through one or more relationships. Teenagers may appear rebellious, oppositional, or insubordinate to the family members, but actually they are simply negotiating the difference between the influence of family and a peer group of alternative persuasion where biological and social needs are being met. Drugs are harmful, physically in most cases, but they also arouse and stimulate the nervous system producing a biologically based "high." There are powerful biological and social factors at work in such a circumstance. It is always a smoother transition from childhood to adulthood when the teenager is enmeshed in peer groups closely linked to the traditions of a family of origin. Caring parents will typically make an effort to provide their children with opportunities to find social comfort by means of the neighborhoods, schools, churches, clubs, social organizations, friendships, or other groups of family affiliation.

So choice is more about relationship flow than what goes on in one's head. We literally bump into relationships which may engage or repel us as we move through life (Maturana called this "purposeless drift"). Those relationships can change our trajectory and move us closer or further from the traditions of our families of origin. So a better term for individual choice from a postmodern perspective is social trajectory. Social trajectory is influenced by relationships that surround us, as prior flow through the web of interaction affects every connection of current involvement.

"Right" choice is connection to a set of relationships that facilitates physical health, survival, and fit within a supportive and caring community.

There are, however, situations where an individual may be placed in a position where it appears he or she is forced to decide one way or another. A parent, for example, may communicate to a rebellious teenager involved in the drug culture, "You stop using drugs, or you leave my house!" Or a male concerned over the influence of another male on his lover may communicate to the lover—"Stop seeing him!" Or a more concrete example: we may have two attractive purchase options, and we must choose one. In these cases, more than any others, the decision process appears to disappear into one's head. I argue otherwise. In fact, a good portion of my most recent career efforts have gone to present an alternative view of decision making. I have argued that what appears to be a decision in one's head is actually a socially constructed and biosocially compelled act (Cottone, 2001).

My model of decision making brings the decision out of the head, so-to-speak, and into the realm of social interaction. It is the "social constructivism model." Decisions occur through past or present interaction, in the processes of "consensualizing," "negotiating," and "arbitrating." Decisions occur when we are faced with competitive truths [bracketed absolutes].

When a parent gives a drug-using teenager an ultimatum, the teenager then must choose. The choice will in the end be made on the levels of attraction or repulsion within the context of relationships of influence. The drug culture will be powerful in this regard. Drugs engage the biological system—they stimulate and arouse the senses. They produce a "high" which is a great feeling, and drugs are often social lubricants for those with stiff or rusty social skills. They are often associated with fulfillment of sexual needs. They connect one, at first, to a fun, exciting, and arousing community. It takes much time for one to recognize the seedy side of the drug culture. Drugs are coming from someone who is connected to the criminal element. For the family to "win" in this situation, there must be positive, healthy, stimulating relationships within the family and around the family of origin.

What appear to be decisions in one's head will be the attraction or repulsion of impinging biological and social factors. In most cases, there will be much interaction around such decisions with people on both sides of the choice. Typically people on both sides will make their best cases in an attempt to influence the decision maker. Decisions are never made in isolation—past and present relationships are always influential. Decisions are not in the head—they are in the array of inter-action leading to an action. A decision always is a consensual act, as one operates within the bracketed absolutes of one or more "truths."

Chapter Conclusion

Beneficence and non-maleficence are historically rooted ethical principles that fit nicely into the postmodern scheme. Beneficence relates to the promotion of good, helping others in need, and collaboration and cooperation to mutual benefit. Non-maleficence relates to avoiding wrongdoing, selfish acts, or harm. When faced with a choice, our ethical community directs us to avoid acting in a maleficent way. In the end, the positive ethic of the human spirit is viewed as contagious—the type of contagion that a positive psychology of religion represents. It is incumbent upon this and future generations to spread the word of the benefit of doing good and avoiding harm to others. Acting with others, joining together, to establish healthy, supportive, caring communities is the postmodern equivalent of a decision to do good and to avoid evil. Decision making, from a postmodern perspective, is the process of socially constructing actions. Decision making involves consensualizing, negotiating, and arbitrating competitive truths [bracketed absolutes]. Decision making is never an individual process.

What is Enlightenment from a Postmodern Perspective?
A Dialogue
A student of postmodern religion addresses her teacher:

Student: "What is the meaning of enlightenment from a postmodern viewpoint?"

Teacher: "Why do you want to know this?"

Student: "Because I have observed some people who appear content, satisfied, and at peace. They have an attractive countenance."

Teacher: "The concept of 'enlightenment' is a culturally embedded term. We find the concept as a goal and as a process fully explored only in a few of the major religions."

Student: "I have studied the concept from several religious points-of-view, but I am very curious how a postmodern thinker views enlightenment."

Teacher: "How would you use your knowledge of the postmodern view of enlightenment?"

Student: "I would be able to address these issues with other postmodern thinkers and explain enlightenment to those who inquire about postmodernism."

Teacher: "So you would use your knowledge to do good and not to do harm? You would not claim superiority over others, if I tell you the meaning of postmodern enlightenment?"

Student: "I seek the answer only as a means of study and as a foundation to communicate with others. I will not use my knowledge to do harm to others ... to discriminate against or oppress those who do not understand or achieve enlightenment."

Teacher: "That said, I will teach you what I have learned from others. Postmodernism is always about relationships, so 'enlightenment' is not inside a person; rather it is a distinction by others about a person."

Student: "You mean it is not a state of being."

Teacher: "It is a process—an interpersonal process. It begins with a distinction in one's language, one's culture, and one's religious tradition that 'enlightenment' exists. Then it is nurtured in a relationship between a teacher of the tradition and a student."

Student: "So it is a process and not a state of being."

Teacher: "Yes, it is an interpersonal process. There is no enlightenment unless some others are able to distinguish it in their relationships with one they define as 'enlightened.'"

Student: "So one never knows on one's own if enlightenment has been attained."

Teacher: "That is true from a postmodern perspective. We only know things in relationships."

Student: "But I want to know what an enlightened person looks like as I relate to him or her—what would postmodernism say about an enlightened one's appearance?"

Teacher: "I can give you one answer, but its truth will depend on your agreement and not with its nature as fact."

Student: "At least tell me one point-of-view, so I may agree or disagree."

Teacher: "An enlightened one in the postmodern tradition would be distinguished from one who would use knowledge to exploit others for the gain of a few. An enlightened one would share ideas and would teach well a philosophy and a method of loving relations. Others would follow, not because they would be forced to, but because they would want to. For them, the message of the enlightened one would resonate, and they would agree that enlightenment had been attained; it is in that agreement that enlightenment would exist. As a student of postmodernism, is that description meaningful?"

Student: "Yes, teacher, I can agree. Thank you. I understand now."

Chapter Ten

Living with a Belief in an Eternity

This Chapter:
- Proposes that eternal life is established through a network of loving relationships.
- Endorses the idea that eternal life can result from procreation or responsible loving care of children.
- Proclaims that one's relationships are greater than one's self.

I want to reap the benefits of allegiance to the Jewish God. I want to love as Jesus loved and experience the guiding hand leading me to heaven. I want to submit to Allah and enter paradise. I want to follow Buddha's method and achieve nirvana. I want to be reincarnated into a higher caste. I want all of these, not one at a time, but all together at the moment of my death.

This may sound selfish or even sarcastic, but the question stands, "Why not?" Why can't someone experience all that is promised by all major religions at the time of death?

Proponents of specific religions would probably argue that there is only one truth—and that truth is represented by each proponent's religion. If there is only one truth, then there can only be one promise of faith—one outcome for having lived a good life. But there are ways one can enter the promised land or the ideal state (of being) from outside of the practice of religion. For example, in the Christian tradition, there is the external forum (you follow church rules and you win big in the end) or the internal forum (you win because you were a good person and God himself likes you, even if you were not a member of his church). So there are ways one can cross the religious bound-aries and still experience the benefits assigned typically to believers. There might be hope for the Dalai Lama, if he faces the Christian god at his death. And perhaps (one can't be sure), Mother Teresa achieved an "enlightenment" of sorts, akin to Buddhist nirvana. But why must we maintain a provincial attitude? Can't we see eternity in another light—one that crosses the boundaries of religions?

Atheists do not believe in an afterlife. They, like proponents of all belief systems, seek to promote a set of principles to live by: (a) believe that there is no god; (b) act as if there is no eternal life; (c) seek to communicate with other non-believers to spread the word of atheism, and (d) convince others that they should behave a certain way, not because of fear of what will happen in the afterlife, but for concern about what will happen in life. Atheism meets the criteria for a belief system. It is acting with others as if some socially defined concept (atheism) represents truth.

A postmodern critique of atheism would go something like the following. First, atheism is a universal absolute truth claim: "There are no gods" (Maisel, 2009). As with all universal and absolute truth claims, those that do not believe are viewed in a negative light. You are either with us or against us (there is no in-between with a universal absolute truth claim). So Christianity condemns those who do not believe Jesus Christ is the "only begotten son of God" (John 3:18), and Islam promises "unbelievers, the fire of hell" (Sura IX: 60), as examples. Because atheists believe that their view is scientific, and that atheism is justified based on data, they define non-believers as intellectually challenged or intellectually dishonest. They operate purely from a modernist objectivist viewpoint. Dawkins (2006), in *The God Delusion*, is a good example. He presents scientific "facts" as evidence of faulty belief in a deity. Dawkins obviously is not a postmodern thinker. He reifies science, and he does not understand the postmodern stand that scientific truths are influenced by the rules of the scientific community. Scientific truths exist within the context of a community of scientists, and from a postmodern perspective, they do not constitute universal truth claims (see Gergen, 2001, who made a detailed comparison of modernist and postmodernist science in psychology). Scientific understanding, like all understanding, is within bracketed absolutes. The scientific constants in nature, from a postmodern perspective, will change, because the "constants" are not outside of the relationship to the observer; the constants are in relationship to what an observer can experience. Our senses and our measurement instruments will evolve and change, and so too will what modernist thinkers hold as constants. So atheists, as a general rule, take an unyielding position on the non-existence of god, act from a stance of intellectual superiority, and criticize non-atheists as non-scientific or intellectually dishonest.

A final criticism of atheism is that it hedges a non-moral position. The science that atheists reify is a science that is supposed to be value neutral. It is supposed to be non-moral. Atheism, as a belief system, is not logically or necessarily associated with an ethical stance. An atheist, based on atheism alone, is no more right or wrong to kill and steal than to value life and the property of others. One can never know, by another's claim to atheism, whether that person subscribes to a code of ethics. Dawkins (2006) made the claim: "There is a consensus about what we do as a matter of fact consider right or wrong: a consensus that prevails surprisingly widely. The consensus has no obvious connection with religion" (p. 298). And then, Dawkins presented a "New Ten Commandments" which he believed reflected atheist morality. The first is: "Do not do to others what you would not want them to do to you." The second is, "In all things, strive to cause no harm." And the list goes on. Dawkins must be kidding! The fact that he sought and presented a list of atheist "Ten Commandments," and then promoted ethical standards that are some of the most religiously established ethical principles on earth (e.g., the "Golden Rule"), identifies him as a person who is steeped in religious culture and tradition. His arguments for a moral atheism distinct from religion are less than credible. There are no secular ethics that emerge from languages and cultures that are enmeshed in religious traditions—that is the postmodern perspective. Atheism, and the modernist science at its foundation, are non-moral. So atheists who seek to align with a moral philosophy must find it in some other community, because atheism has nothing to offer in this regard. Arguments by other atheists that a moral code may be found through something akin to an individual, subjective, moral conscience (cf., Maisel, 2009) fail from a postmodern perspective, because there is no individual moral conscience in postmodern thought as presented here.

When an atheist dies, all that his or her atheist colleagues know with certainty is that his or her life is completely finished in this world. There are no alternative states of being—no heaven, hell, paradise or nirvana. There is no coming back through the lives of others. It's over. The colleagues of the atheist know that the person no longer exists. This is their shared belief. As with all beliefs, it has validity within its community of believers.

And if the atheist suffered a harsh life, one of pain and suffering, what reason was there to live? If an atheist experiences disability, a shortened painful life due to disease, the fate of the poor and downtrodden, torture or trauma, then what hope is there? The message that he or she carries forward is "This life is all there is." And if one's life is horrible, then suffering is the best that one can expect. One leaves no legacy for others in pain (especially children) when the message one carries is a message of no hope beyond suffering.

Life is a one-way street. And for some of us, the street is a rocky road. Atheism leaves a legacy of despair for those who are the most unlucky among us. You live a painful life, and you die.

Atheism, although vulnerable to a postmodern critique, does have its place. It will likely be attractive to relatively healthy, secure, modernist-thinking intellectuals and those who act outside of culturally imbedded moral standards.

So maybe I don't have to have it all. But at least give me some hope that there is meaning in my life. Give me some hope that I can live in some way past the life that I live on this earth, no matter how much pain or despair I experience. I need others to believe with me that my life is worthwhile. I need others to acknowledge that my existence is valuable. I need others to share a belief that we are in this together, and that I will affect them as they will affect me, even after life. I need to know that my words and memories of me will live on and will affect people in positive ways. I want an afterlife.

Maybe I already have one. I experience something like reincarnation every time I look in my daughter's eyes and see my own eyes staring back at me. I experience a sort of heaven or paradise as I see my son as a grown man entering fatherhood. I speak of god when I lay next to my disabled son, sharing a loving moment with him, and asking, "Do you feel Jesus' presence with us here?" And when he answers, "Yes," I know that his god is with us. Then I say, "You know Jesus promised us eternal life." And he says, "Yes, Dad, I know." I experience something like nirvana when I feel connection and unity with all that I assume exists and will exist beyond me. There is an afterlife. There is a life beyond. It is in relationships. This is the message of postmodernism. This is the message of those who have gone before us.

Jesus lives through the *New Testament*. Allah lives through the *Koran*. The Jewish prophets today teach a powerful message. Buddha's students follow him to this day—those that study his words and actions and aim to achieve what he achieved. The Hindu gods exist among their followers practicing with an eye, a third eye, looking toward a better life. The great ones live.

There is no clearer message that there is an afterlife. This is their message. And those who follow live through the lives of the great ones, so long as their message survives.

Postmodernism acknowledges a belief in eternity. It accepts that a belief in eternity is as valid as any other. And since the message of eternity offers hope to some with little hope, it persuades. Nothing is more convincing than the message of the ancient religions in this regard.

Poor Zeus. He was such a powerful god. And the souls of Mount Olympus...are they remembered? Do we know what their lives meant? To live in eternity takes more than a doctrine. It takes more than a set of principles. It takes enduring relationships. It takes a community of adherents passing the message and the method to future generations.

I once visited the Mayan ruins in the Yucatan peninsula of Mexico. I learned that sacrifices were made to the Mayan gods. The best athletes and healthiest women were sacrificed to the gods—killed in ritual sacrifice to the gods that were praised by the Mayans. The very best of the Mayan offspring willingly (or perhaps unwillingly) gave their lives for the cause of god worship. It is no wonder that the Mayan culture no longer exists as anything close to what existed in the ancient times. Although there are many reasons for the demise of the Mayan empire, killing one's healthiest and strongest offspring is a sure formula for cultural extinction. And yet, we can walk among the ancient Mayan ruins and see incredible monuments to these gods. We know that for those people, praise of their gods occupied much of their lives and effort, but to little historical avail. While at the sites, I could visualize the events that occurred in my imagination, but I could not feel the presence of those that went to their deaths. I knew little of their culture and little of their beliefs. I could not understand their states of mind. I could not enter into a consensual frame with them, as my world and their world, my words and their words, would not intersect. To reiterate, eternity takes more than holding to a principle or doctrine. It takes enduring relationships, hope, and a credible message communicated to a culture's future generations.

There are two sure bets for survival after one's death: (1) procreation or care of children in need, and (2) adherence to long-lasting principles that one can embrace and pass forward, with confidence, that the principles will enhance the survival of like kinds. We live on through our children, and we live on through the community and cultural standards that survive and facilitate the human condition. And how are we fairing? To live in eternity, one must be forward looking. One must have confidence that one's work and effort pass forward, and that the future generations will look back and have a record of the good acts that led to their well-being. We should not be sacrificing our offspring to the gods of selfishness. We should be thinking of the future.

If you want to live forever, put your effort in the future. One's future in eternity is ensured by daily efforts to build an extended network of loving relationships. If you want to experience eternal joy, then place your bets on the joy of those that follow. Make your mark. Communicate ideals for better living. Document historical and contemporary means for insuring a better day. And if you cannot have or decide not to have children of your own, then you have a very special role in assisting others in need and in demonstrating the power of relationships. We are all brothers and sisters, and we should celebrate our connection in the present and in the future. Just like in the 2000 movie *Pay it Forward*, where a young man, when challenged by his teacher to do something to change the world, begins to pay good deeds forward (not just repaying the good deed doer) by doing something in response that positively affects three other people. Paying it forward becomes contagious, as he begins to affect his own circle of friends and family in a positive way, and he also begins to affect an ever growing circle of people with which he is connected. People should know that life is valuable and they will not be abandoned. Pay the message forward.

The message may be passed in words, in music, in art, in dance, in theatre, and by action. The message must be pervasive, attractive, and engaging. It must be a positive message about life and living. It must build on our inclination to cooperate, to collaborate, and to act together to face the challenges that life naturally brings.

That message can begin by establishment of a set of principles for living life to its fullest. That message is inherent in our social needs. The message is grounded upon a relational view of reality and of the human condition. That message is embodied in the human spirit.

We recognize now the power of relationships in affecting what we believe and what we hold as "truth." So there is consolation to good Christians that they will, at the time of their deaths, in the physical or emotional embrace of other believers, experience a connection to life after death. They will live on through the Christian legacy. The people that follow them will hold the deceased to be present in their lives and in their actions. They will be, as Jesus on the cross, an everlasting example for all surviving Christians. They will be models of what is good in a Christian life and in Christian death. Of this, Christians can be assured.

This is true of all of the ancient religions. I have no doubt that Hindus experience reincarnation by observing the similarities of character across the generations. I believe that Buddhists experience enlightenment and may achieve a higher state of being by following the Buddha's path. I know with certainty that Jewish people benefit for themselves and for their children by pleasing their god in life and in death. I feel the comfort dying Muslims experience as they are raised by Allah to paradise. There is no doubt for me on those matters, because for each religious community there is absolute truth in the ideal shared in life and in death.

Postmodernism does not negate an afterlife, it just locates it within a community of believers. It accepts the atheist alternative as a valid and acceptable standard, as it recognizes atheism as a system of belief akin to other religions. But the postmodern position is that an afterlife exists through one's connection to one's community. *To accept that one lives on through relationships is to accept that there is something greater than oneself.*

Individuals have no sole choice in an afterlife, or, for that matter, in religious affiliations. Their culture, education, history, and traditions speak through them. Their religion is a manifestation of their relationships within a religious community and tradition.

Just as one's relationships change sometimes drastically over a lifetime, one's religious affiliation, and one's belief or lack of belief in an afterlife can change. The religious landscape is in constant flux, just as people flow between and among relationships. When one examines the population as a whole, there are sometimes dramatic changes within and across religions. People are capable of redefining truth if given an opportunity to enter into dialogue with others on the topic of belief. Rather than being static or "set in stone," religious affiliation is fluid and constantly changing. Even within religions there are developments that have doctrinal implications, as, for example, the Episcopalian acceptance of women and gay ministers.

As one's religion changes, so too does one's conception of truth and an afterlife.

Chapter Conclusion
The message of postmodernism is that no matter where one starts, or where one ends, one lives in perpetuity through religion by means of enduring relationships (both biological and

social), hope, and a message that compels future generations. One's relationships are greater than one's self.

Can You Create a "Thing" Through Socially Constructing a Reality?
A Dialogue
A student of postmodern religion addresses her teacher:

Student: "I am still a bit confused about the meaning of socially constructing a reality. Does that mean that people can consensualize that a brick or any 'thing' exists, and therefore it exists and has substance to them?"

Teacher: "No. You have to be exact in your language as a postmodern thinker. People do not socially construct a 'reality' or a 'thing' through consensualizing. Consensualities don't create things, they only construct understanding of shared experiences."

Student: "So it's not really about whether a brick exists or not."

Teacher: "That's correct. But it is about what meaning is given to the brick that people perceive and talk about together."

Student: "Can you give me an example?"

Teacher: "Sure. Consider people sitting around a large table in a conference room. In the middle of the table is a bowl of fruit. One of the people at the table states, 'I'm so hungry. Is that fruit for public consumption?' Another person says, 'I'm not sure it is real fruit—it might be wax fruit.' The hungry person says, 'It looks so real.' A third person reaches over and picks up an apple and a banana from the bowl. He says, 'Hey, it isn't real, but it's not wax either. It feels and smells like rubber.' So the others all feel and smell the fruit and they come to agreement that it is, in fact, rubberized decorative fruit. At that moment, the group socially constructed an understanding of their shared experience through consensualizing. They didn't create the rubberized decorative fruit, but they did understand it through their inter-action. It became a bracketed absolute truth through their inter-action."

Student: "So does that mean all groups would do the same?"

Teacher: "No. Consider another group of individuals in an isolated underdeveloped part of the world. They may have no language for, or experience with, wax or rubberized fruit, so they would have to socially construct new meaning around their fruit bowl experience. They might define it as a 'hoax,' or a 'joke,' or a 'threat' if they have a language for such concepts. To them, meaning will come from their interaction in their language and cultural context."

Student: "I understand. Different groups can construct different meanings around similar experiences."

Teacher: "That's correct. And that's the premise behind postmodern religion. People, for example, don't invent a god, but they interpret their experiences to mean that a god exists. One group's interpretation of god may be different from another group's interpretation of a god, even though their experiences may be very similar. The defined god is understood by them within the confines of their group interaction and from the perspective of their cultural context."

Student: "Well can't just one person have an experience and then individually construct meaning on his or her own?"

Teacher: "Not if language is involved. Once one involves language, one has entered the social domain. The interpretation of an experience in language will always reflect the traditions and representations of one's relationships and culture. In other words, one's understanding through language will be culture bound and reflective of one's past relationships. To escape language would return humans to a pre-linguistic or pre-symbolic state, where religion does not exist."

Student: "But can't one person find emptiness in his or her own experience?"

Teacher: "If one seeks 'emptiness,' one is already in language, as the concept of 'emptiness' can only be understood through interaction in the social domain. Seeking emptiness is an Eastern tradition, for example. We can't individually own any concept (such as 'emptiness') that is shared through language."

Student: "I think I am understanding. So we can't socially create 'things.' And we can't invent meaningful language outside of relationships. So when we apply language as a means of understanding, we do it with all the relationship history that preceded the words."

Teacher: "Yes, and belief is acting with others as if some socially defined concept represents truth."

Student: "Thank you, Teacher."

Part III:

Science and Religion in the Postmodern Era

Chapter Eleven

Science, Belief, and Belief Science

This Chapter:
- Presents a postmodern view of science.
- Concludes that science does not define universal truth.
- Purports that science and religion both represent communities of understanding.
- Gives a definition of belief—acting with others as if some socially defined concept represents truth.
- Defines religious and scientific truth in context, but not as objective or subjective truths.

When I first began to understand science in school, it was an exciting time. Science gave answers to questions. Science was factual. Science could unravel the mysteries of the universe. There were principles in nature—rules and laws that defined and predicted real events.

I learned about Isaac Newton's law of gravity and apples falling from trees. Gravity...now there's a concept that applies to everyone's life all the time. What fun to study the laws of nature. And what fun to study the likes of Isaac Newton, Leonardo da Vinci, Benjamin Franklin, Madame Curie, Albert Einstein, and Thomas Edison.

While in college, though, I learned of another way to look at science. I was introduced in the 1970's to a postmodern view of science. Where science in the modern era dealt with discovering or identifying concrete facts and laws of nature, postmodern science deals with relationships—specifically relationships among ideas and among scientists.

For me, the hero of the postmodern view of science was an

historian of science named Thomas Kuhn. In 1962, Kuhn wrote a book entitled *The Structure of Scientific Revolutions*. In his book, Kuhn argued that science is not a smooth process of discovering and accumulating knowledge. Rather, science is a competition of ideas, and it is also a competition between groups of scientists. Each group of scientists proposes a point-of-view, a hypothetical theory believed to explain nature or to predict natural events. Good science, according to Kuhn, pits one view against another.

Back to Newton. Who could argue with his law of gravity? His formulas work. You drop a cannonball off a building, and if you put the right values in the formula, it will tell you how long it will take the ball to fall a certain distance. Newton's law is simple, straightforward, and a fact of nature. So why challenge it. It is not arguable. Or is it?

Einstein argued. He argued that although Newton's law applied in the context of the earth's locale, it did not work away from the earth at very large distances. He argued that the law of gravity was a local truth. He proposed a different theory. He stated that there was not a force pulling things down; rather, he argued that space was literally warped by mass, curved, and he proposed that objects that appeared to be falling were actually moving through curved space. That is an idea that will "give one pause." It seems ridiculous to consider that space is warped, because here on earth we see things falling straight. But Einstein's ideas mean that when we look up at the stars in the sky, the stars are not really where they appear to be! Space is all curvy out there, because there are massive stars and planets that affect what appears to be straight. So a star in the sky straight ahead is likely somewhere else!

Einstein's theory was controversial, but astronomers recognized they could prove it during a total eclipse of the sun. If they took photographs during the eclipse and little dots of stars showed up in places they were not supposed to be, that meant that the light of the stars traveled a crooked path due to the mass effect of the sun and moon. The light of the stars would literally curve because space was curved as the light traveled by the sun and moon (and astronomers could see the starlight because the sunlight was blocked by the moon). It took years for astronomers to get a good test of the idea, but finally, after several failed attempts (clouds, wars, and such impeded early attempts), they were able to get good data. Einstein's theory was supported.

But support for his theory was not proof. It took many years for experiments to catch up with the theory. In the end, Einstein's ideas garnered support not only from experimental data, but from a new generation of scientists. His formula was more complex than Newton's, but it applied to very big (cosmic) and very small (subatomic) contexts, as well as on the surface of the earth. As the older scientists holding an opposing viewpoint passed on, the new generation embraced Einstein's ideas. There was a scientific revolution.

We learn from Kuhn that there is no "proof" of a theory, but only experimental support for the theory. Kuhn explained that all scientific revolutions take time, because they are not about facts, but they are about people and ideas. Ideas in science are never understood in isolation. They are always understood in opposition to other ideas. For example, in the past scientists argued that light was particles; others argued that it was waves. A third point-of-view holds that it could be either particles or waves, depending on the means of measurement. So what is light? One answer is: "It depends." From the postmodern view the answer "it depends" fits all questions.

Kuhn's ideas sparked a controversy themselves. There are those who argue the "modernist" viewpoint—facts are facts and science is truth. But Kuhn's theory states that truth is always from a particular perspective and there are competing truths. In the end, the validity of a scientific truth is established by its enduring and useful application across observable phenomena.

Its veracity comes from people in relationships who apply the ideas or come together to challenge the ideas with new and revolutionary possibilities.

So science is not really about truth. It is about possibilities. Science, like all understanding, comes from people making distinctions and then acting around those distinctions.

Studying ideas like Kuhn's I began to get a bigger picture. Now the scientific truths I learned in science classes in childhood became debatable. With debate, one enters the social realm.

Science and Religion

If science is debatable, then religion is even more debatable. Here is a revolutionary idea that is open for debate: science and religion are the same. The postmodern revolution proposed that all truths are in relationships, not outside. It is irrelevant whether we make a distinction that a truth is scientific or religious. All truth involves agreement among people who subscribe to the principles of the truth and follow the principles with action.

Although the historical distinction between religion and science has been a useful one in the modern age, it has caused problems too. Science was viewed as addressing facts in the physical world, and religion was viewed as addressing facts in the spiritual world. Not too long ago there was persecution of scientists on religious grounds. Galileo's case is one of the saddest. They put him in prison as a heretic, all because he proposed that the earth was not (and therefore humans were not) the center of the universe. Wouldn't Galileo have preferred to live in the postmodern era, where he might be heard at least without fear of religious retribution? Religion does shine a bright light, but it makes a dark shadow. The scientists of the past and present who suffered or suffer censure, imprisonment, or ostracism are victims of a distinction that is oppressive. It is perturbing to hear about mullah's running Iranian universities.

It is even more perturbing to hear Pope Benedict XVI declaring to Catholic educators in the United States, "that any appeal to the principle of academic freedom in order to justify positions that contradict the faith and the teaching of the Church would obstruct or even betray the university's identity and mission..." One has to wonder what the consequences will be, because any academic scientist worth his or her salt would be well served to flee a university that restricts freedom of thought.

Postmodernism proposes that the distinction between science and religion is just that—a distinction. But postmodernism also holds that the interpersonal processes—the actual social activities that occur in religion and in science—are the same. Religion and science both involve people holding to a truth and acting on the truth.

Einstein said: "Science without religion is lame; religion without science is blind." Today a religion that does not embrace science and science that does not embrace religion are equally dangerous. There is no fear in learning that we have evolved from apes, unless one holds that a competitive religious truth (creationism) is absolute and that all people must subscribe to that doctrine. There is no fear in carrying out controversial experiments, unless those experiments show no respect for the value of human life or the environment. There is danger in both science and religion if they are practiced without adherence to some very basic principles: life is valuable, the free flow of ideas is valuable, and social justice must prevail.

I no longer view science and religion in opposition. I think they address different domains of human interaction distinguished historically by the terms "physical" and "spiritual," but they are both still within the realm of human relations. Where others distinguish religious truth versus scientific truth, I see only people in relationships.

Belief Science

I have been intrigued by the study of the science of belief at least since 1974 when I wrote a college paper on belief as a useful concept in uniting theories of counseling and psychotherapy. In that paper, I defined belief as "acting as if something defined is." Today, after over 30 years of study, I have revised that definition. Belief is acting with others as if some socially defined concept represents truth.

The study of belief and the believing process has been a long journey for me. And psychology and counseling have been the vehicles that have carried me on this journey. The journey neared completion with recognition of the idea of "bracketed absolutes," the foundation of what I call "belief science."

Bye Bye Objectivism

It was easy for me to give up an objectivist's view of religion—a view that there is only one "right" answer in religion—one "god" figure from which all truth flows.

In America, we live in a pluralistic society in a multicultural world. Recognizing that there are different perspectives was not an intellectual stretch for me. Americans live in a free society, so we hear about Islam, Hinduism, Buddhism, Judaism, Christianity, atheism/agnosticism and other religions on a daily basis. These religions are described on TV and in the other media regularly. So giving up objectivism was easy, because it was easy to observe that other faiths had some validity to believers. But I was bothered most by the other option—"subjectivism" (or individual relativism). Subjectivism implies that each person can know a personal truth—a truth that is unique to the person alone. It means that somehow through some magical means unknown by humankind, a truth is experienced outside of language and inside the person. It had to be outside of language, because language is in the social domain and would take the subjective truth away from the individual and locate it within the socio-linguistic tradition. As Gergen (2001) argued, "Language is inherently a by-product of human interchange. There can be no private language" (p. 805). Hypothetically, one could experience pure subjectivity if he or she were somehow raised in a world without human symbolic communication. There actually have been cases of humans raised by animals, and it appears they are permanently negatively neurologically affected; they have significant difficulty establishing meaningful civilized interaction with other humans. The hypothetical idea that someone could have an internal individual subjective truth outside of language rendered the person to the likes of the animal world. It essentially removed the person from the human realm and brought him or her backward to the pre-linguistic or non-symbolic world of the animal kingdom. As my puppy lies beside me as I meditate, he may be experiencing a great feeling, something akin to nirvana. But he cannot share it linguistically with me. He is in a purely relative mode—pure subjectivity. Once we leave language, we leave our human-ness behind. I once told this to a friend who said I had it "all wrong." He argued that we are most human when we leave language. My response to him was: "Who told you so?" He didn't want to admit it, but he read it in a book on Eastern philosophy. He was arguing the "Eastern point-of-view." If you take a stand in language on some matter, even if that stand paradoxically is that one can transcend language, you operate within the social domain (which is counter to the idea of subjectivity). I believe that humans would have to relinquish all symbolic communication to achieve a perfect state of subjectivity, and then, to what end?

Selflessness is Plural

It was while studying Buddhist philosophy along with academic studies of postmodernism that I began to understand a third way of addressing the subjective-objective continuum. When one practices Buddhist meditation, one does it according to a philosophy and with a method in mind. Buddhism is a process and an outcome that is communicated typically through written works or by means of a teacher-student relationship. One learns of Buddhist philosophy by reading Buddhist texts or the works of the Tibetan Dalai Lama, or by entering a relationship with a teacher of the art. Even in this very reflective style of practicing religion, one cannot escape doctrine. There is language at its root. Buddha was a teacher, living into old age educating others about his method, and, importantly, teaching the concept of enlightenment through his example. Buddhism is a culture. It is a human activity, as even in finding selflessness one finds connection to one's Buddhist family.

Studying the works of the cognitive biologist Humberto Maturana and the social psychologist Kenneth Gergen also facilitated a conversion. Maturana's concept of "objectivity in parentheses" helped me to recognize that there is an objectivity aside from pure objectivity. There is a relativism that is not relative to personhood. There is a way to view beliefs as reflecting objectivity within the boundaries of group interaction. When one is communicating in language, one is not alone. Gergen called this "communities of shared intelligibility." When one acts in accordance with a concept, one enters consensus with those who defined the concept. When one reads the *Koran*, one is in relationship with Muhammad. When one reads the *Bible*, one is in relationship with the Christian god through the authors of the books and gospels. When there is a book in hand or live social interaction, there is relationship. As readers, you are in a relationship with me at this very moment. You may or may not like what I have to say, but at this moment, there is something between us. That something is our relationship, and it is manifest in this communication.

When two people act in a coordinated fashion around some concept, there is consensualizing. Consensualizing is a process of acting and negotiating a socially defined truth with at least one other person. What would have happened if John the Baptist would not have believed Jesus was the Messiah? What if John would have railed against Jesus stating that he was an imposter? What then? What if Bonnie Nettles would not have agreed with Marshall Applewhite about their role in "Heaven's Gate?" It takes two to know a truth. It takes at least two.

For me, recognizing the social aspect of "truth" was huge. It was the variable in the equation I could not fully discern back in 1974. We literally socially construct our understanding of the world. It's not an isolated individual process, and neither is it simply discerning a fact about an objective world. Knowledge is in relationships. Knowledge is in the social matrix. It's not objective. It's not subjective. It is real only within the context of human interaction.

The concept of "bracketed absolutes" helped me to negotiate the objective-subjective impasse. The key was recognizing that truths defined within social contexts and enlivened through interaction become absolutely true, unquestionable facts to those who are involved in the process.

What is common among all religions is a community of believers. The community is crucial. People believing together can accomplish great things. This was a positive message that I learned from Catholicism. The Roman Catholic Church is outstanding in its ability to rally people to a religious cause. It is powerful in its sense of community. Many Catholic parishes, building on traditions of love, hope, and caring for others in need, are able to enlist the support, dedication, and energy of a cadre of believers. Food pantries are stocked. The homeless are given shelter. The elderly are given loving care. The poor are given educational assistance, and on and on. I saw this as a youth in my own church. And as an adult I have been awestruck by the commitment of religious people, across many religions, to devote themselves to socially responsible causes, and all in the name of a religious principle. We live in belief, and belief lives in its community.

Chapter Conclusion

The study of belief science has returned me to my roots as a child raised in a religious tradition. It took me back to a formula about belief—that belief is acting as if something defined is— and it helped me to revise the equation. Belief is acting with others as if some socially defined concept represents truth. This is the postmodern definition. This is one conclusion to one long journey in the study of belief science.

Who Will Change Their Viewpoint or Adopt a Postmodern Position on Religion?
A Dialogue
A student of postmodern religion addresses her teacher:

Student: "I'm finally beginning to understand the precepts of postmodern religion and the implications for human under- standing and interaction. But who will ascribe to such a position?"

Teacher: "Some people already are acquainted with postmodern ideals, and if these ideas resonate, then it will be easy for them to consider a formal alignment with postmodern religious tenets. Others who ascribe to what they believe to be a universal truth will have more difficulty. People who are adherents of other religious traditions and actively associate or communicate with others of the same persuasion likely will have some serious doubts about the validity of postmodern ideals. Some people may even be threatened by postmodern religious ideas, and they may mistakenly represent it as a type of relativism. They may not understand the unique concept of bracketed absolute truths, where truths within a community are viewed as absolute, but from outside a community a truth claim appears relative. This is a common mistake among critics—they argue that postmodernism is relative. Also, some may see postmodern religion as an alternative universal truth claim. But postmodern philosophy, ironically, brackets itself—it does not claim universality—it claims only its place beside other possible truth claims that people can accept or reject depending on their social, linguistic, and cultural traditions. Postmodern philosophy makes no claim of superiority—it just provides one way to view the world of religion and it welcomes those who can agree. Someone who subscribes to postmodern religious ideals must be able to accept that there are multiple truths at many levels operating in this world, each having validity within its community of believers. The survivability of postmodern religious philosophy, therefore, does not come from a threat to believers or non-believers, but to a positive message that compels people to expand the supportive community of believers."

Student: "But why would someone switch religions to join those of a postmodern ilk?"

Teacher: "People shouldn't change religions for change's sake. Some people are ignorant of or ignore the negative philosophies or histories of their religions. Often people accept blindly the ritual practices and traditions that are passed down through generations. If they find solace in their religions, and, if for whatever reason, they ignore their religions' dictates to condemn or to hate others, or to discriminate against certain people, then there is little harm in their affiliation to a religion such as those of the ancient traditions. But if they are intellectually honest and read and truly understand the doctrine of their religions, and they recognize and embrace the negative aspects and messages of their beliefs, then they likely will find that they are directed to experience anger or hostility toward others or justification to discriminate against others. When this occurs, their religion becomes detrimental to self and/or others, and adherents should certainly make the effort to re-examine their beliefs and to put them in perspective. It is also possible that once people in certain groups analyze the foundational beliefs of their religions, they may recognize that they are marginalized or rejected by their own religions. Religions that are highly restrictive of behavior, that limit freedoms of adherents, or that discriminate against certain groups will likely find a flight of adherents to more positive, inclusive belief systems. Postmodernism provides a foundation for a positive, inclusive religious philosophy. And of course, some people may already subscribe to an inclusive and accepting system of beliefs that serves them well and that is not detrimental to self or others, in which case they would be friendly and accepting of those of the postmodern or other persuasions."

Student: "Do you see the postmodern religious movement as viable and growing?"

Teacher: "Yes, I am optimistic that postmodern religious ideals will prevail, as they will engage the inbred human spirit that has served humanity from the prehistoric through the modern eras. As people learn and understand postmodern philosophy as applied to religion, I believe they will embrace postmodern principles. I view postmodern religion as a seed that will grow into a viable, lively, and enduring plant with many flowering branches."

Student: "Thank you, Teacher."

Chapter Twelve

Is This "The Truth?"

This Chapter:
- Makes an appeal for readers to join in a postmodern view of faith.
- Proposes that religion should lead the way to a new world order.

As an academic, I have learned to organize my ideas, to write them in presentable form, and to disseminate them to an appropriate audience. This book is my effort not only to address the shortcomings of the ancient religions in the postmodern era, but to construct an alternative philosophy. This is my way of sharing with you, the reader, my most profound understanding of my experiences.

I view the postmodern movement as the most significant intellectual development in my lifetime. It has the potential to affect human relations in a dramatic way. It has given me an advanced understanding of psychology and religion. Postmodernism shines a bright light upon all religions. It provides a model for comprehending how people come to believe so completely and devoutly that they will give their lives in defense of their beliefs. It inhabits a philosophical position off of the objective-subjective continuum, providing an alternative way to define theories of understanding (where objectivity is located within the parameters of human interaction). It defines a relational reality, where "things" are viewed as perceptual phenomena for the transmission of relationships. It gives us a new term, "consensualizing," which reflects the process whereby people come to believe together—acting with others as if some socially defined concept represents truth. It defines "bracketed absolutes"—truths that look relative to outsiders, but are held as unquestioned facts by insiders of a community. Postmodernism takes understanding out of the limits of concrete thinking, the limits set during the modern era. We now have a way to comprehend knowing beyond thinking that either the map is the territory or that knowledge resides within isolated individuals. This is my attempt to communicate the postmodern ideal.

The postmodern era, which allows for instantaneous communication to a large populace, makes transmission of religious ideas, such as the postmodern ideal, much easier. Religious doctrine is no longer spread by word of mouth. It is no longer communicated by oral narrative. In the postmodern era, churches and religions have websites and addresses on personal and business World Wide Web spaces. The message of religion travels near the speed of light across the planet. We no longer need storytelling and personal meetings to communicate on religious ideas. We can post the ideas for many to read in a chat room or on a blog on the Internet. Today it is estimated that there are thousands of religions on this planet. Postmodern religion must take its place aside its many brethren. The message must be spread so others may at least consider what postmodernism has to offer religion.

But you may ask, "Why would someone spread the postmodern word by criticizing the most prevalent religions on earth?" I think some people may question my motives or whether I have a score to settle. I assure you, I have written this book without anger. I respect all religious traditions and would be a hypocrite to believe the ideas in this book are "better" than those of other religious documents. Or some might think that I have a "god complex." There are plenty of stories of megalomaniacs trying to find a following. As a psychologist, I try to keep my narcissism in check. In fact, I've taken my share of "whacks" for writing about religion. It certainly hasn't been an "ego boosting" experience. My Roman Catholic wife, for example, reminds me often that I am "going to hell." I've asked her to join me, but for some reason, she resists. There are some things love cannot conquer. All-in-all, I see myself as a regular guy, an idealist who wants to share some good ideas, and someone who also has a penchant to organize thoughts and to put them to pen.

The ideas I have presented, which I incorporate through the term "Belief Science," have no special status. They are not "the truth." They are simply representative of "a truth." If people agree with the ideas presented as Belief Science, then the ideas will have some role in affecting human relations within and outside the group of believers. People who are not Belief Scientists are in no way condemned or viewed as inferior or defective. They just hold a place that for them has meaning—their niche—which is acceptable from the position of Belief Science. Belief Scientists accept many truths, while modeling ethical interaction.

We can heed the warnings of postmodernism. We understand that under certain relational circumstances people are vulnerable and may come to believe they have special standing over others. People can come to believe easily that their truth is "the truth." They can learn to be discriminating, or to target others, or to condemn. When "a truth" is held to be universal instead of local, those individuals that do not subscribe are in danger of harm or discrimination. But if the postmodern message is heeded, we may begin to agree to a new set of rules for engagement—rules that can lead to consensualizing about principles for optimal interaction and establishment of a better place for our progeny. The positive psychology movement is salient in this regard.

The future is bright. I have confidence that the human spirit will prevail. I do not believe that the end of civilization is imminent. I believe that when our planet comes to its natural end, we will be long gone to new places to live. I have faith in human intelligence and the human spirit. We have the motivation to work together to survive. What scares me most is our tendency to believe uncritically and to generalize local truths as universal truths. Ethics and intelligence have the potential to supersede the aggressive instincts, but people must be willing to listen to opposing viewpoints and to discern rules for living collaborative and cooperative lifestyles. There is little room for selfishness, as we are all connected in a very intricate web of human interaction.

So the message of postmodernism resounds. It is a position that not only explains religions as local and bounded [bracketed] absolutes, but it also explains itself as a local and bounded [bracketed] truth. There are other equally valid ways to understand the world. Legitimacy is only a matter of consensus through time. The validity of any idea comes from its pervasive and enduring application to human understanding and to human events. History has shown that certain ideas may have the potential to influence human relations in such a way as to enhance the lives of people and to increase the likelihood of survival of the species. Other ideas live short lives. Concepts such as democracy, the freedom to share ideas, and free enterprise are examples of concepts that have served humanity well. Unfortunately, the large world religions have not kept pace with the needs of people in the postmodern era. They are non-democratic and authoritative, and in many cases anti-science.

The world has shrunk as a result of scientific advancement, and there is an increased need for collaboration, cooperation, and intelligent co-action. The world reaction to the 2008 financial crisis is a good example of what can be accomplished when people come together to solve problems. Many nations responded with coordinated action to limit the damage that resulted from selfishness. Although the results are not yet known, the fact that there was a concerted effort, nearly worldwide, with quick communication and coordinated activity to address a massive financial crisis, is a sign that the postmodern ideal is functional and operative in human relations.

Today we know a few things that our predecessors did not know. We know that people respond in healthier ways to reward than punishment. We know that threat has negative consequences. By working together and negotiating differences, we excel. We know that we are all connected and that the self is a vestige of the modern era (the psychological equivalent of the appendix). We know that we can communicate with each other, even worldwide, almost instantaneously. And we know that differences among us can be viewed not as threats, but as challenges. We believe that challenges can be met with commitment and open communication. This is the postmodern hypothesis—we are all in this together and we have the potential to achieve and to thrive by embracing each other fully and with reasonable rules of interaction. By accepting the postmodern hypothesis, we have the potential to move forward and to create an enduring legacy for our children.

We must stand for a positive psychology of religion. Religion must lead the way.

Epilogue

What is fair is fair. I believe everyone who has read these pages ought to have an opportunity to critique these ideas, as I have critiqued the ancient religions. I welcome you to visit the website of the Church of Belief Science at:

www.churchofbeliefscience.org

Enter through the "forum" page for discussions of all religions, or enter the Belief Science forum to critique these and other ideas associated with the Church of Belief Science. I post a blog frequently and would love to hear from you.

I wish you well on your journey, and thank you for letting me share these ideas with you.

Bibliography and References

American Psychiatric Association. (1994). *Diagnostic and statistical manual of mental disorders, 4th edition*. Washington, DC: Author.

An-Nawawi's Forty Hadiths (English Translation) (2009, October 21). Retrieved from http://www.iiu.edu.my/deed/hadith/other/hadithnawawi.html.

Bateson, G. (1972). *Steps to an ecology of mind*. New York: Ballantine.

Bateson, G. (1979). *Mind and nature: A necessary unity*. New York: Bantam.

Cottone, R. R. (1992). *Theories and paradigms of counseling and psychotherapy*. Needham Heights, MA: Allyn & Bacon.

Cottone, R. R. (2001). The social constructivism model of ethical decision making in counseling. *Journal of Counseling and Development, 79*, 39-45.

Cottone, R. R. (2008). *The Church of Belief Science: A complete guide to philosophy and practice*. Cottleville, MO: Author.

Cottone, R. R., & Tarvydas, V. M. (2007). *Counseling ethics and decision making, 3rd edition*. Columbus, OH: Merrill Prentice Hall.

"Dominus Iesus": On the unicity and salvific universality of Jesus Christ and the Church. (2000, August 6). Retrieved August 21, 2007 from http://www.ewtn.com/library/CURIA/CDFUNICI.HTML.

Freud, S. (1900). *The interpretation of dreams*. Standard ed. Vol. 4. NY: W. W. Norton.

Freud, S. (1901). *The psychopathology of everyday life*. Standard ed. Vol. 6. NY: W. W. Norton.

Garrett, J. T., & Garrett, M. T. (2002). *The Cherokee full circle: A practical guide to ceremonies and traditions*. Rochester, Vermont:

Bear and Company.

Gergen, K. J. (1985). The social constructionist movement in modern psychology. *American Psychologist, 40*, 266-275.

Gergen, K. J. (2001). Psychological science in a postmodern context. *American Psychologist, 56*, 803-813.

Kohn, S. C. (1994). *A life of the Buddha*. Boston, MA: Shambhala.

Kuhn, T. (1962/1970). *The structure of scientific revolutions.* Chicago, IL: University of Chicago Press.

Mahabharata. (1999). As retold by Krishna Dharma. Badger, CA: Torchlight.

Maturana, H. R. (1978). Biology of language: The epistemology of reality. In G. A. Miller & E. Lenneberg (Eds.), *Psychology and biology of language and thought*. New York: Academic Press.

Maturana, H. R. (1980). Biology of cognition. In H. R. Maturana & F. J. Varela, *Autopoiesis and cognition: The realization of the living*. Boston: D. Reidel. (Original work published in 1970.)

Maturana, H. R., & Varela, F. J. (1980). Autopoiesis: The organization of the living. In H. R. Maturana & F. J. Varela, *Autopoiesis and cognition: The realization of the living*. Boston: D. Reidel. (Original work published in 1973.)

Mitchell, S. (2000). *Bhagavad Gita: A new translation.* New York: Three Rivers Press.

Neihardt, J. G. (1932/2004). *Black Elk speaks.* Lincoln, NE: University of Nebraska Press.

Nietzsche, F. (1968). The Antichrist. In W. Kaufmann (Ed. & Trans.), *The portable Nietzsche* (pp. 565-656). New York: Penguin. (Original work published in 1888).

Schachter, S., & Singer, J. E. (1962). Cognitive, social, and physiological determinants of emotional state. *Psychological Review, 69*, 379-399.

Schmitz, C. D., & Schmitz, E. A. (2008). *Golden anniversaries: The seven secrets of successful marriage.* USA: Briarcliff.

Seligman, M. E. P., & Csikszentmihalyi, M. (2000). Positive

psychology: An introduction. *American Psychologist, 55*, 5-14.

Simon, R. (1992). A frog's eye view of the world: An interview with Humberto Maturana. *One on One* (pp. 89-97). Guilford: NY.

Skinner, B. F. (1938). *The behavior of organisms*. NY: Appleton-Century-Croft.

Skinner, B. F. (1953). *Science and human behavior*. NY: McMillan.

Szasz, T. S. (1974). *The myth of mental illness*. New York: Harper & Row.

Talmud (Babylonian): Tractate Shabbath, Folio 31a (2009, October 21). Retrieved from http://www.come-and-hear.com/shabbath/shabbath_31.html.

The Dhammapada. (2007). New York: Random House Modern Library Edition.

The Koran. (1993). New York: Ivy Books.

The New American Bible. (1987). Nashville: Thomas Nelson.

The Tibetan Book of the Dead. (2000). Boston, MA: Shambhala.

The Torah: The Five Books of Moses. (1962). Philadelphia, PA: The Jewish Publication Society.

Udanavarga. F. Bernhard (editor, 1965). (January 2006 Sanskrit Version 2.1) Retrieved October 26, 2009 from http://www.ancient-buddhist-texts.net/Buddhist-Texts/S1-Udanavarga.

The Upanishads. (2007). Tomales, CA: Nilgiri Press of the Blue Mountain Center of Meditation.

Watson, J. B., & Rayner, R. (1920). Conditioned emotional reactions. *Journal of Experimental Psychology, 3*, 1-16.

BOOKS

O is a symbol of the world, of oneness and unity; this eye represents knowledge and insight. We publish titles on general spirituality and living a spiritual life. We aim to inform and help you on your own journey in this life.

Visit our website: http://www.o-books.com

Find us on Facebook:
https://www.facebook.com/OBooks

Follow us on Twitter: @obooks